Catch a Wave

**Written by Wallie Winholtz,
Kathy Cramer, and Sherry Twyman.
Humorous Asides and Random Cartoons
Courtesy of B. K. Hixson**

Catch a Wave

Copyright © 2002
First Printing • August 2002
B. K. Hixson

Published by Loose in the Lab, Inc.
9462 South 560 West
Sandy, Utah 84070

www.looseinthelab.com

Library of Congress Cataloging-in-Publication Data:

Hixson, B. K.
    Catch a Wave/B. K. Hixson, Wallie Winholtz,
Kathy Cramer, & Sherry Twyman
        p.   cm.-(Loose in the Lab Science Series)

    Includes glossary and index
        ISBN 0-9660965-5-x
    1. Sound-experiments-juvenile literature. [1. Sound-
Experiments 2. Experiments] I. Wallie Winholtz II. Kathy
Cramer III. Sherry Twyman IV. Loose in the Lab V. Title
VI. Series
QP441.D54   2002
534.078

Printed in the United States of America
Surf's Up, Dude!

Dedication

For the Faculty, Staff, and Kids @ Hermosa Valley School

Hugs and kisses to Dee Strange and Linda Zimmermann, my two co-conspirators in many "projects." And a warm thank you to Connie Ridgeway, our fearless leader who supported science 110%. Jackie, thank you for all the great parties and for keeping us Irish. Kiyo, Connie, Connie, and Kim—Thanks for sharing your ideas and helping me understand anklebiters a little better. Mr. "Downtown" Bobby Brown—Thanks for all the great stories and helping me with my many projects. Kris—The programs were great and better theatre cannot be found at that level anywhere. And Daryl—Getting to know you opened my eyes to a whole new world. I am sure that I have left someone out and I apologize but thank you to all.

I have very fond memories of the staff, faculty, parents, and especially the kids that let me experiment with my ideas in the lab. Thanks for the laughter, applause, and love that you gave in such great abundance.

Nothing but the best!

Bryce

Acknowledgments

There are always a lot of thank-yous that need to be passed out when a book gets published and this one is no exception. On top of the list are my co-authors, Wallie Winholtz, Kathy Cramer, and Sherry Twyman, the infamous Missouri Gang, a cadre of middle school teachers from Kansas City who submitted the basic ideas that provided the foundation for this book. Their complete works can be found in two teacher-oriented resource books titled _Surf's Up, Sound's On!_ (Grades 2-3) and _Good Vibrations!_ (Grades 5-6), available down the line.

As for my educational outlook, the hands-on perspective, and the use of humor in the classroom, Dr. Fox, my senior professor at Oregon State University, gets the credit for shaping my educational philosophy while simultaneously recognizing that even at the collegiate level we were onto something a little different. He did his very best to encourage, nurture, and support me while I was getting basket-loads of opposition for being willing to swim upstream. There were also several colleagues who helped to channel my enthusiasm during those early, formative years of teaching: Dick Bishop, Dick Hinton, Dee Strange, Connie Ridgway, and Linda Zimmermann. Thanks for your patience, friendship, and support.

Next up are all the folks that get to do the dirty work that makes the final publication look so polished but very rarely get the credit they deserve. Our resident graphics guru "Kris Barton" gets a nod for scanning and cleaning the artwork you find on these pages, as well as putting together the graphics that make up the cover. A warm Yankee yahoo to Eve Laubner our editor who passes her comments on so that she and Kathleen Hixson can take turns simultaneously proofreading the text while mocking my writing skills.

Once we have a finished product, it has to be printed by the good folks at Advanced Graphics—Michael Williams, Matt, and the crew—so that Louisa Walker, Kent Walker, Tracy St. Pierre, and the Delta Education gang can market and ship the books, collect the money, and send us a couple of nickels. It's a short thank-you for a couple of very important jobs.

Mom and Dad, as always, get the end credits. Thanks for the education, encouragement, and love. And for Kathy and the kids—Porter, Shelby, Courtney, and Aubrey—hugs and kisses.

Repro Rights

There is very little about this book that is truly formal, but at the insistence of our wise and esteemed counsel, let us declare: *No part of this book may be reproduced or utilized in any form or by any means, electronic or mechanical, including photocopying, recording, or by any information storage and retrieval system, without permission in writing from the publisher.* That would be us.

More Legal Stuff

Official disclaimer for you aspiring scientists and lab groupies. This is a hands-on science book. By the very intent of the design, you will be directed to use common, nontoxic, household items in a safe and responsible manner to avoid injury to yourself and others who are present while you are pursuing your quest for knowledge and enlightenment in the world of physics. Just make sure that you have a fire blanket handy and a wall-mounted video camera to corroborate your story.

If, for some reason, perhaps even beyond your own control, you have an affinity for disaster, we wish you well. *But we, in no way take any responsibility for any injury that is incurred to any person using the information provided in this book or for any damage to personal property or effects that are directly or indirectly a result of the suggested activities contained herein.* Translation: You're on your own. Great speakers may make your ears bleed, teeth clatter, and hair stand on end but no one told you to stand in the front row.

Less Formal Legal Stuff

If you happen to be a home-schooler or very enthusiastic school teacher, please feel free to make copies of this book for your classroom or personal family use—one copy per student, up to 35 students. If you would like to use an experiment from this book for a presentation to your faculty or school district, we would be happy to oblige. Just give us a whistle and we will send you a release for the particular lab activity you wish to use. Please contact us at the address below. Thanks.

Special Requests
Loose in the Lab, Inc.
9462 South 560 West
Sandy, Utah 84070

Table of Contents

The National Content Standards (K-4)

Sound is produced by vibrating objects. The pitch of the sound can be varied by changing the rate of vibration.

The National Content Standards (5-8)

Energy is a property of many substances and is associated with heat, light, electricity, mechanical motion, sound, nuclei and the nature of a chemical.. Energy is transferred in many ways.

The 10 Big Ideas About Sound & Corresponding Labs

1. Sound is produced when objects vibrate.

2. Sound is also produced when gas expands rapidly.

3: Sound is a form of energy and can be converted to or from other sources of energy.

4: Sound travels as one of two kinds of waves-longitudinal (compression) or transverse. The parts of these waves can be identified as the crest, trough, amplitude, node, and antinode.

5: The pitch of the sound can be varied by changing the rate of the vibration. The rate of vibration can be varied by changing the length or thickness of a vibrating object. The faster an object vibrates, the higher the pitch it produces.

Table of Contents

6: Sound waves can be transmitted through solids, liquids, and gases but never through a vacuum.

7: Sound waves can be reflected.

8: Sound waves can be collected and amplified.

9: Sound waves can be absorbed. If the object absorbing the sound is resonant with the object that is producing the waves, that object may also produce and amplify the same sound.

10: Variations in wave patterns can produce phenomena like bangs, explosions, sonic booms, and the Doppler Effect.

Who Are You? And . . .

First of all, we may have an emergency at hand and we'll both want to cut to the chase and get the patient into the cardiac unit if necessary. So, before we go too much further, **define yourself**. Please check one and only one choice listed below and then immediately follow the directions that follow *in italics*. Thank you in advance for your cooperation.

I am holding this book because ...

    ___ A. I am a responsible, but panicked, parent. My son / daughter / triplets (circle one) just informed me that his / her / their science fair project is due tomorrow. This is the only therapy I could afford on such short notice. Which means that if I were not holding this book, my hands would be encircling the soon-to-be-worm-bait's neck.

    Directions: Can't say this is the first or the last time we heard that one. Hang in there, we can do this.

    1. Quickly read the table of contents with the worm bait. The Big Ideas define what each section is about. Obviously, the kid is not passionate about science or you would not be in this situation. See if you can find an idea that causes some portion of an eyelid or facial muscle to twitch.

    If that does not work, we recommend narrowing the list to the following labs because they are fast, use materials that can be acquired with limited notice, and the intrinsic level of interest is generally quite high.

How to Use This Book

2. Take the materials list from the lab write up and page 181 of the Surviving a Science Fair Project section and go shopping.

3. Assemble the materials and perform the lab at least once. Gather as much data as you can.

4. Go to page 158 and start on Step 1 of Preparing Your Science Fair Project. With any luck you can dodge an academic disaster.

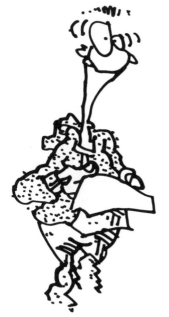

___ B. I am worm bait. My science fair project is due tomorrow and there is not anything moldy in the fridge. I need a big Band-Aid, in a hurry.

Directions: Same as Option A. You can decide if and when you want to clue your folks in on your current dilemma.

___ C. I am the parent of a student who informed me that he/she has been assigned a science fair project due in six to eight weeks. My son/daughter has expressed an interest in science books with humorous illustrations that attempt to explain sound and associated phenomena.

Who Are You? And . . .

Directions: Well, you came to the right place.

A. The first step is to read through the Table of Contents and see if anything grabs your interest. Read through several experiments, see if the science teacher has any of the more difficult materials to acquire like tuning forks, convection carafes, and some of the chemicals, and ask if they can be borrowed. Play with the experiments and see which one really tickles your fancy.

B. After you have found and conducted the experiment that you like, take a peek at the Science Fair Ideas and see if you would like to investigate one of those or create an idea of your own. The guidelines for those are listed on page 168 in the Surviving Your Science Fair section. You have plenty of time so you can fiddle and fool with the original experiment and its derivations several times. Work until you have an original question you want to answer, and then start the process listed on page 245. You are well on your way to an excellent grade.

___ D. I am a responsible student and have been assigned a science fair project due in six to eight weeks. I am interested in sound and, despite demonstrating maturity and wisdom well beyond the scope of my peers, I too still have a sense of humor. Enlighten and entertain me.

Directions: Cool. Being teachers, we have heard reports of this kind of thing happening but usually in an obscure and hard-to-locate town several states removed. Nonetheless, congratulations.

Same as Option C. You have plenty of time and should be able to score very well. We'll keep our eyes peeled when the Nobel Prizes are announced in a couple of years.

How to Use This Book

___ **E. I am a parent who home schools my child/children.** We are always on the lookout for quality curriculum materials that are not only educationally sound but kid and teacher friendly. I am not particularly strong in science but I realize it is a very important topic. How is this book going to help me out?

Directions: In a lot of ways we created this book specifically for home schoolers.

1. We have taken the National Content Standards, the guidelines that are used by all public and private schools nationwide to establish their curriculum base, and listed them in the Table of Contents. You now know where you stand with respect to the national standards.

2. We then break these standards down and list the major ideas that you should want your kid to know. We call these the Big Ideas. Some people call them objectives, others call them curriculum standards, educational benchmarks, or assessment norms. Same apple, different name. The bottom line is that when your child is done studying this unit on sound you want them to not only understand and explain each of the 10 ideas listed in this book, but also be able to defend and argue their position based on experiential evidence, hands-on science, that they have collected.

3. Building on the Big Ideas, we have collected and rewritten 50 hands-on science labs. Each one has been specifically selected so that it supports the Big Idea that it is correlated to. This is critical. If the kids do the science experiment, see it, smell it, touch it, and hear it, they will store that information in several places in their brains. When it comes time to comprehend the Big Idea, the concrete hands-on experiences provide the foundation for building the idea, which is quite often abstract. Kids who merely read about harmonic nodes, resonance, and pitch, notice the transfer of energy from one source to another, or overhear someone describing the Doppler Effect, are trying to build abstract ideas on abstract ideas and quite often miss the mark.

Who Are You? And . . .

For example: I can show you a recipe in a book for chocolate chip cookies and ask you to reiterate it. Or I can turn you loose in a kitchen, have you mix the ingredients, grease the pan, plop the dough on the cookie sheet, slide everything into the oven and wait impatiently until they pop out eight minutes later. Chances are that the description given by the person who actually made the cookies is going to be much better based on their true understanding of the process, **founded in experience.**

4. Once you have completed the experiment there are a number of extension ideas under the Science Fair Extensions that allow you to spend as much or as little time on the ideas as you deem necessary.

5. A word about humor. Science is not usually known for being funny even though Bill Nye The Science Guy, Beaker from Sesame Street, and Beakman's World do their best to mingle the two. That's all fine and dandy but we want you to know that we incorporate humor because it is scientifically (and educationally) sound to do so. Plus it's really at the root of our personalities. Here's what we know:

When we laugh ...
a. Our pupils dilate, increasing the amount of light entering the eye.
b. Our heart rate increases, which pumps more blood to the brain.
c. Oxygen rich blood to the brain means the brain is able to collect, process, and store more information. Big I.E.: increased comprehension.
d. Laughter relaxes muscles, which can be involuntarily tense if a student is uncomfortable or fearful of an academic topic.
e. Laughter stimulates the immune system, which will ultimately translate into overall health and fewer kids who say they are sick of science.
f. Socially, it provides an acceptable pause in the academic routine, which then gives students time to regroup and prepare to address some of the more difficult ideas with a renewed spirit. They can study longer and focus on ideas more efficiently.
g. Laughter releases chemicals in the brain that are associated with pleasure and joy.

6. If you follow the book in the order it is written you will be able to build ideas and concepts in a logical and sequential pattern. But that is by no means necessary. For a complete set of guidelines on our ideas on how to teach home school kids science, check out our book, <u>Why's the Cat on Fire?</u> <u>How to Excel at Teaching Science to Your Home Schooled Kids</u>.

How to Use This Book

___ F. **I am a public/private school teacher** and this looks like an interesting book to add ideas to my classroom lesson plans.

Directions: It is, and please feel free to do so. However, while this is a great classroom resource for kids, may we also recommend two other titles that can be found in two teacher oriented resource books titled <u>Surf's Up, Sound's On!</u> (Grades 2-3) and <u>Good Vibrations</u> (Grades 5-6).

These two books have teacher preparation pages, student response sheets or lab pages, lesson plans, bulletin board ideas, discovery center ideas, vocabulary sheets, unit pre tests, unit exams, lab practical exams, and student grading sheets. Basically everything you need if you are a science nincompoop, and a couple of cool ideas if you are a seasoned veteran with an established curriculum. All of the ideas that are covered in this one book are covered much more thoroughly in the other two. They were specifically written for teachers.

___ G. **My son/daughter/grandson/niece/father-in-law** is interested in science, and this looks like fun.

Directions: Congratulations on your selection. Add a gift certificate to the local science supply store and a package of hot chocolate mix and you have the perfect rainy Saturday afternoon gig.

___ H. **After years of going to Grateful Dead concerts we were wondering, which we do a lot these days, if there was any way to recover the range of hearing, clarity of pitch, and full color of the audio rainbow using your toilet paper kazoo.**

Directions: Nope. Try the audiologist and some Ben & Jerry's Cherry Garcia ice cream.

Lab Safety

Contained herein are 50 science activities to help you better understand the nature and characteristics of sound as we currently understand these things. However, since you are on your own in this journey we thought it prudent to share some basic wisdom and experience in the safety department.

Read the Instructions

An interesting concept, especially if you are a teenager. Take a minute before you jump in and get going to read all of the instructions as well as warnings. If you do not understand something, stop and ask an adult for help.

Clean Up All Messes

Keep your lab area clean. It will make it easier to put everything away at the end and may also prevent contamination and the subsequent germination of a species of mutant tomato bug larva. You will also find that chemicals perform with more predictability if they are not poisoned with foreign molecules.

Organize

Translation: Put it back where you get it. If you need any more clarification, there is an opening at the landfill for you.

Dispose of Poisons Properly

This will not be much of a problem with labs that use, study, produce, and manipulate sound. However, if you happen to wander over into one of the many disciplines that incorporates the use of chemicals, then we would suggest that you use great caution with the materials and definitely dispose of any and all poisons properly.

Practice Good Fire Safety

If there is a fire in the room, notify an adult immediately. If an adult is not in the room and the fire is manageable, smother the outbreak with a fire blanket or use a fire extinguisher. When the fire is contained, immediately send someone to find an adult. If, for any reason, you happen to catch on fire, **REMEMBER: Stop, Drop, and Roll.** Never run; it adds oxygen to the fire, making it burn faster, and it also scares the bat guano out of the neighbors when they see the neighbor kids running down the block doing an imitation of a campfire marshmallow without the stick.

Protect Your Skin

It is a good idea to always wear protective gloves whenever you are working with chemicals. Again, this particular book does not suggest or incorporate chemicals in its lab activities very often. However, when we do, we are incorporating only safe, manageable kinds of chemicals for these labs. If you do happen to spill a chemical on your skin, notify an adult immediately and then flush the area with water for 15 minutes. It's unlikely, but if irritation develops, have your parents or another responsible adult look at it. If it appears to be of concern, contact a physician. Take any information that you have about the chemical with you.

Lab Safety

Save Your Nosehairs

Sounds like a cause celebre, LA style, but it is really good advice. To smell a chemical to identify it , hold the open container six to ten inches down and away from your nose. Make a clockwise circular motion with your hand over the opening of the container, "wafting" some of the fumes toward your nose. This will allow you to safely smell some of the fumes without exposing yourself to a large dose of anything noxious. This technique may help prevent a nose bleed or your lungs from accidentally getting burned by chemicals.

Wear Goggles if Appropriate

If the lab asks you to heat or mix chemicals, be sure to wear protective eye wear. Also have an eye wash station or running water available. You never know when something is going to splatter, splash, or react unexpectedly and it is better to look like a nerd and be prepared than schedule a trip down to pick out a seeing eye dog. If you do happen to accidentally get chemicals in your eye, flush the area for 15 minutes. If any irritation or pain develops, immediately go see a doctor.

Lose the Comedy Routine

You should have plenty of time scheduled during your day to mess around but science lab is not one of them. Horseplay breaks glassware, spills chemicals, and creates unnecessary messes. Things that parents do not appreciate; trust us on this one.

No Eating

Do not eat while performing a lab. Putting your food in the lab area contaminates your food and the experiment. This makes for bad science and worse indigestion. Avoid poisoning yourself and goobering up your labware by obvserving this rule.

Happy and safe experimenting!

Recommended Materials Suppliers

For every lesson in this book we offer a list of materials. Many of these are very easy to acquire and if you do not have them in your home already you will be able to find them at the local grocery or hardware store. For more difficult items, we have selected, for your convenience, a small but respectable list of suppliers who will meet your needs in a timely and economical manner. Call for a catalog or quote on the item that you are looking for and they will be happy to give you a hand.

Loose in the Lab
9462 South 560 West
Sandy, Utah 84070
Phone 1-888-403-1189
Fax 1-801-568-9586
www.looseinthelab.com

Delta Education
80 NW Boulevard
Nashua, NH 03061
Phone 1-800-442-5444
Fax 1-800-282-9560
www.delta-education.com

Nasco
901 Jonesville Ave.
Fort Atkinson, Wisconsin 53538
Phone 1-414-563-2446
Fax 1-920-563-8296
www.nascofa.com

Ward's Scientific
5100 W. Henrietta Road
Rochester, New York 14692
Phone 1-800-387-7822
Fax 1-716-334-6174
www.wardsci.com

Educational Innovations
362 Main Avenue
Norwalk, Connecticut 06851
Phone 1-888-912-7474
Fax 1-203-229-0740
www.teachersource.com

Frey Scientific
100 Paragon Parkway
Mansfield, Ohio 44903
Phone 1-800-225-FREY
Fax 1-419-589-1546
www.freyscientific.com

Edmund Scientific
101 E. Gloucester Pike
Barrington, NJ 08007
Phone 1-800-728-6999
Fax 1-856-547-3292
www.edmundscientific.com

Sargent Welch Scientific Co
911 Commerce Court
Buffalo Grove, Illinois 60089
Phone 1-800-727-4368
Fax 1-800-676-2540
www.sargentwelch.com

The Ideas, Lab Activities, & Science Fair Extensions

Catch a Wave • Winholtz, Cramer, Twyman, & Hixson

Big Idea 1

Sound is produced when objects vibrate.

Ring Around the Rim

The Experiment

This experiment provides the opportunity for you to learn about sound vibrations and make an obnoxious, irritating noise. What a great way to start a book.

When you dampen your finger-tip and rub it gently around the rim of a wine glass, it will begin to emit a high-pitched sound. This continual ringing sound will soon begin to drive the neighborhood cat into a frenzy, sending it up the nearest tree. The exact mechanics of that will be covered in an entirely different book. But for now, 50 experiments to antagonize your neighbor ...

Materials

3   Wine glasses, same size
1   Finger
    Water

Procedure

1.   Fill one wine glass a third full, the second, two-thirds full, and the third glass, almost completely full.

2.   Dampen your forefinger and rub it gently around the rim of the first glass. As you rub, you will notice that the glass will begin to emit a faint hum. You are setting up a standing wave. Either slow down or speed up a little, and the sound will get louder.

3.   Experiment with the different levels of water. Each glass will produce a different pitch, and when you get really good, you can tune an entire scale of wine glasses and play a song. The cat is already headed over the back fence.

How Come, Huh?

When you rub your finger around the edge of the glass, the glass begins to vibrate back and forth, and this causes the air above the water to vibrate back and forth, as well. The less water there is in the glass the longer the sound waves and the lower the pitch will be. By the same contrast, the more water in the glass the higher the sound waves will be.

The main thing that you want to take out of this lab is that sound is produced when an object vibrates.

Science Fair Extensions

1. As you make the ringing sound with your glass, place a drop of food coloring in the water. Watch the results. You should be able to see the vibrations as the color mixes with the water.

2. Add some sawdust or pencil shavings to the water. Watch the particles move on the surface of the water as the glass vibrates.

3. Create a neighborhood symphony. Nab a group of your friends and teach them how to make wine glasses vibrate. Once they get the hang of it, fill the glasses with different levels of water and tune your orchestra.

4. Try different liquids in the glasses. Now you're messing with density. Try syrup, oil, Jello, glycerin, rubbing alcohol, etc.

Tuning Fork Waves

The Experiment

Inexpensive tuning forks are used to demonstrate how fork size affects pitch. A large Papa-Bear-sized fork, medium Mama-Bear-sized fork, and small Baby-Bear-sized fork are tapped with a rubber mallet. Feel free to add a little mood music, such as "Good Vibrations" by the Beach Boys.

Predict the pitch that will be made by tapping three sizes of tuning forks with a rubber mallet. Then use your mallet to tap away and find out if your prediction was right.

Materials

3   Tuning forks
    (different frequencies)
1   Bowl
    Water

Procedure

1. Hold one of the tuning forks by the lowest point on the handle and tap it gently on your knee.

2. While it's vibrating, bring the tuning fork up to your ear. You will be able to hear a distinct tone.

3. Fill the bowl with water. Whap the tuning fork on your knee for a second. Then place the tuning fork upside down in the bowl and observe what happens.

4. Repeat this procedure with each tuning fork. Note the pitch, as well as the size of the wave created in the bowl by each different instrument.

How Come, Huh?

If you looked carefully at the metal tines of the tuning fork, you could see them vibrating back and forth very quickly. Sound is actually measured in vibrations, or cycles per second, and these tuning forks produce vibrations that are in the hundreds-of-cycles-per-second range. Any vibration you see would be a blur. That is why we stick the fork in the water. The fork transfers its vibrational energy to the water, which is thicker than air. Because of its thickness, it produces slower waves that are easier to see.

Galileo, an Italian physicist who was fond of dropping metal balls off tall buildings during his lunch hour, was the first to infer that shorter piano strings had a higher pitch because they produced a higher frequency of vibration.

Science Fair Extensions

5. If a piano is available, measure the length of the strings. The relationship between the string length and the pitch of the corresponding keys is an inverse proportion. ➠ short string = high pitch

6. Design other ways, in addition to making water vibrate, to show that tuning forks are vibrating. To do this, you will need to transfer the energy from the fork to something else. (Think of how drums produce sound.)

Soap Film Vibrations

The Experiment

This experiment will allow you to actually see sound waves as they are produced by a stereo speaker. The medium for seeing these sound waves will be a thin film of soap that is suspended between two straws. As you hold this film up to the speaker, you will be able to see the soap film vibrate in response to the music that you choose to play.

Materials

1   Bottle of liquid detergent, Dawn or Joy
1   1-oz. bottle of glycerin
1   1-gallon tub
1   1-cup measure
1   Teaspoon
2   Straws
1   Roll of cotton string
1   Pair of scissors
1   Stereo w/speaker
1   Music CD
    Water

Procedure

1. Fill a one-gallon plastic tub almost to the top with warm tap water. Mix in one cup of Dawn or Joy liquid soap. (For a reason known only to the soap gods, these two brands produce the best soap films for this kind of experiment.) Stir well.

2.   Add one teaspoon of glycerin and mix the solution thoroughly. The longer you let this mix stand, the stronger and better the film, the better the bubble will be. Waiting a couple of hours is great; waiting a couple of days is better.

3.   Cut a 40" length of cotton string from the roll. Thread both straws onto the string, and tie the string off. When you are done, you should have a soap film holder like the one pictured at the right.

4.   Holding the straws together, dip them in the bubble solution. Still holding them together, pull them out of the solution and then separate them. This produces a large, square film of soap. Practice making the film of soap until you are comfortable with the process.

5.   Now it's time to plug in your favorite music and crank up the CD! Pick something that has a good bass beat. If you have a button on your boom box that allows you to amp up the bass, push it in. Start with the volume low and increase it slowly, watching the soap film as you do.

GLYCERIN

SOAP

WATER

TUB

Soap Film Vibrations

6. Dip the straws into the soap solution and pull them apart to stretch the soap film. Hold the soap film up to the stereo speaker, as shown in the illustration at the right, and observe what happens to the film as the sound is produced by the speaker.

How Come, Huh?

When the speaker receives the electrical signal from the amplifier, a magnet in the speaker causes the cone to vibrate back and forth. When the cone vibrates, it pushes air away from the speaker in waves. As those waves travel out into the room, they bounce into the soap film, which is thin and flexible enough to vibrate easily. This allows us to see sound.

Science Fair Extensions

7. Soap films are very light and flexible, but they also expire very quickly. Try suspending other types of films in front of the stereo speaker. Watch them move when the sound waves hit them. (There are thin plastic films and tissue papers that you may want to use.)

8. Find other sources of sound. If you are measuring the sound waves with soap films, you will have consider the fact that they burst easily. Look for moderate sources of sound.

Puffed Rice Disco

The Experiment

Here's another lab that allows you to see sound waves, or at least the effect of the energy from the sound waves. A stereo speaker is positioned so that the bass cone points straight up. A thin pie tin is placed directly on the bass cone, and a handful of puffed rice cereal grains are placed in the pie tin. When the music is turned up, the sound waves cause the puffed rice to dance.

Materials

1   Stereo w / speaker
1   Music CD
1   Pie tin, 9" to 12"
1   Box of puffed rice

Procedure

1. Flip a stereo speaker on its back so that the bass cone is facing upward.

2. Place a pie tin over the bass speaker and toss a handful of puffed rice grains into the pie tin.

3. Turn the music on, slowly increase the volume, and watch what happens as the sound waves hit the pie tin.

How Come, Huh?

As with the previous experiment, the speaker moves back and forth, pushing against the air to produce sound. The vibrating air hits the bottom of the pie tin. The tin vibrates and transfers some of that energy to the puffed rice. The rice starts to vibrate or dance. (Hey, dancing is in the eye of the beholder, right?)

T. P. Kazoo

The Experiment

A kazoo is an old instrument, probably only one or two twists removed from the blade of grass between the thumb to make noise trick.

Materials

1   Toilet paper roll, empty
1   Cellophane square
1   Roll of cellophane tape
1   X-Acto knife

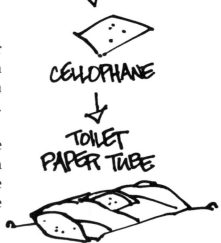

Procedure

1.   Flatten the toilet paper tube. Using the X-Acto knife, cut a small square, about a half inch by a half inch, on the top half of the tube.

2.   Cut a square of cellophane that is roughly three fourths of an inch by three fourths of an inch. Place the cellophane square over the hole and tape it down on all four sides.

3.   Hum into one end of the tube and listen to the sounds that are produced. Squeeze the tube open and closed and see if that affects the sound.

How Come, Huh?

When you hummed into the kazoo, you were producing vibrations from your vocal cords. These vibrations traveled down the tube and pushed on the cellophane, causing it to vibrate and produce its own sound.

Big Idea 2

Sound is also produced when gas expands rapidly.

Thunder Poppers

The Experiment

This is an age-old experiment which also moonlights as a fun birthday-party game, an entertaining student-assembly activity, and a poor-man's cardiac stimulator. A balloon is inflated to near-capacity and is tied off. The balloon is placed under the fanny of the experimenter, who promptly deploys his full weight onto the balloon. The result is a very large bang, or pop. You can do a similar experiment using a paper bag and your hands.

Materials

1   Balloon, 9" round
1   Chair or hard surface
1   Fanny
1   Paper bag, quart size

Procedure

1. Fill a balloon as full of air as possible. (We suggest that you use 9" round balloons because they are very common. However, you can substitute any kind that you can find.) Tie the balloon off.

2. Place the balloon on a chair or other hard surface. Hold it in place with your hand.

3. Plop your bones on top of the balloon. The weight of your body should be sufficient to cause the balloon to pop. If not, keep the balloon on the chair and sit down with greater force.

4. Next, fill the bag with air and twist the neck of the bag to lock the air inside.

5. Hold the bag in one hand, spread your arms out, and bring your two hands together quickly. The bag should burst and the air should rush out. The dog should be going nuts.

How Come, Huh?

When you trapped the air inside the balloon and bag, you created closed systems. Nothing could get into or out of them. When you sat on the balloon, and squashed your bag, you were compressing the air inside each, and putting enormous pressure on the rubber and paper. When the pressure increased to the point where the material could no longer hold the weight, the rubber or paper popped and the air inside expanded rapidly. This rapid expansion of air sent a shockwave, in the form of a pressure wave or giant vibration, into the room. Our ears perceived this as a "boom."

Science Fair Extensions

9. Experiment with different sizes of bags. See if the amount of air inside the bag makes a difference in the boom that is created.

10. Find some plastic bubbly wrap, used to protect packages in shipment. Apply pressure to the bubbles by squeezing or stepping on them. Listen for small booms as you do so.

The Whooping Tube

The Experiment

Acids and metals have never gotten along very well. We are going to take advantage of that fact in this experiment. Dilute sulfuric acid is added to mossy zinc. When the two react, they produce a flammable gas ... and an odor that rivals that found in any end-of-the-year gym locker.

Materials

1   20mm by 150mm test tube
1   1 oz. bottle of 1M sulfuric acid
3   Mossy zinc pieces
1   Book of matches
1   Pair of goggles
    Water

SULFURIC ACID

MOSSY ZINC

TEST TUBE

Procedure

1.   Add enough sulfuric acid to a test tube to fill it to a level of about 2 inches. Drop a couple of pieces of mossy zinc into the acid and observe what happens.

2.   After the reaction has proceeded for about 30 seconds, darken the room. Ask an adult to carefully light a match and hold it near the mouth of the tube. If you look closely, you will see a bright blue flame ignite the gasses at the top of the tube and migrate to the liquid layer. When the flame gets to the liquid layer, the tube will produce a small "whoop."

3.   This reaction will continue for several minutes. Be sure to let the tube have time to recharge (fill with gas). Have an adult relight the tube as many times as is possible.

4.   Turn the lights back on and gently waft the odor that is produced by the reaction. Never stick your nose directly over the tube and snort the gases into your nasal passages.

How Come, Huh?

The acid reacts with the zinc to produce hydrogen sulfide—rotten egg gas. This explains the smell. The hydrogen is flammable, so when the match is introduced into the mouth of the tube, it ignites the gas. The "whoop" was caused by the rushing of hot gas out of the tube, which produced a vibration at the top of the tube when it escaped. Sound being produced by rapidly expanding air, take 3 ...

Science Fair Extensions

11.   Perform the experiments in tubes of different diameters and lengths. You will find that both the diameter of the tube and the distance between the top of the tube and the liquid level factor into the sound that is produced.

12.   Any rapidly burning gas confined in a small space will produce a sound as it is escaping. With the permission of your parents research other flammable gases and explore the possibilities for making noise.

Soda Cannon

The Experiment

You will add vinegar to the bottom of a test tube. You'll then insert baking soda that has been wrapped in a piece of toilet paper into the top of the tube. The whole assembly is stoppered and shaken. As the two chemicals react, the stopper is pushed out of the tube very quickly. What does this have to do with sound, you ask? Simple... As the gas is produced inside the tube, the pressure in the tube increases dramatically. When it gets to the point where the stopper cannot hold back the pressure, the gas inside expands rapidly, producing a "pop."

STOPPER

BAKING SODA IN T.P.

VINEGAR

TEST TUBE

Materials

1   20mm x 150mm test tube
1   #1 rubber stopper, solid
1   1 oz. bottle of white, distilled vinegar
1   Sheet of toilet paper
1   Bottle of baking soda powder
1   Pair of goggles

Procedure

1. Goggles on. You are going to shoot stoppers through the air. Best not to catch one in the eye.

2. Take a single section of toilet paper. Pour a pile of baking soda, roughly the size of a quarter, onto the paper. Fold the toilet paper in half several times, until it looks something like a plug.

3. Hold the test tube in one hand and pour about half an inch of white, distilled vinegar into the bottom of it.

4. Insert the toilet paper plug into the *top* of the tube. Push it in with the rubber stopper. (Be sure you are pointing the stoppered end of the tube *toward* the ceiling and *away* from other kids.) The illustration to the right should give you a good idea of how to assemble your filled tube.

5. Point the tube *away* from yourself and others. Shake it vigorously. There will be a very quick chemical reaction inside the tube, and the stopper will explode into the air. **Be sure you are pointing the tube up and away from yourself and others.**

6. In addition to the stopper shooting up into the air, listen for a small explosion that accompanies the action.

How Come, Huh?

When the carbon dioxide mixed with the vinegar, a huge pile of carbon dioxide gas was produced. If the gas had been allowed to escape out of the top of the tube, the pressure would have been the same. However, the tube had a stopper in it, and that means that the pressure inside the tube increased very rapidly. (Cram a whole bunch of molecules into a small space and then keep adding more and pretty soon everyone wants out!) After the reaction builds up, there are so many molecules inside the tube, they gang up and shove the stopper off the top of the tube. The compressed gas rushes out and *voila'*… we have sound in the form of a bang!

The Burping Bag

The Experiment

We have produced sound by sitting on balloons, smashing paper bags, lighting gases that are flammable in small, enclosed spaces, and compressing gases by virtue of a chemical reaction that resulted in an explosion. Why not have an encore performance of the last idea? Two chemicals will be mixed in a sealed container. When the gas pressure increases to the point where the container fails, we will have a small and very polite explosion of gas.

Materials

1   Measuring cup
1   1 oz. bottle of baking soda powder
1   1 oz. bottle of calcium chloride pellets
1   Resealable baggie
    Water

Procedure

1. Add a half-cup of warm water to the baggie.z If you don't have a measuring cup, fill the bag until there is about an inch of water in it. **Be sure to use warm water. (Using cold water will change the experiment significantly.)**

2. Remove the cap from the calcium chloride bottle and add about one-third of the bottle to the water. Zip the baggie closed and roll the pellets between your fingertips. As the chemical starts to dissolve, you should notice a significant increase in temperature, particularly as you roll the pellets between your fingers.

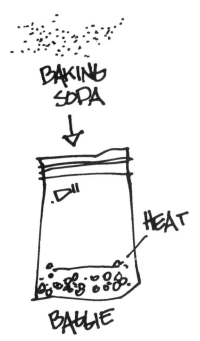

BAKING SODA

HEAT

BAGGIE

3. Open the baggie, quickly add one-third of the bottle of sodium bicarbonate powder and *quickly* zip the baggie closed again. Observe what happens when the chemicals come in contact and react with one another.

4. As the reaction proceeds, hold the baggie up to your ear and listen. The bag will swell with gas until it "pops" along the zipper. You can either close it up and let it collect more gas or …

5. Pour the ingredients down the drain with lots of running water.

How Come, Huh?

When calcium chloride is mixed with water, it splits apart, forming calcium and chloride ions. When this happens, the energy that was holding those atoms together is released as heat. That is why the bag started to feel warm as the reaction proceeded.

GAS EXPANDS

SEAL GIVES

GAS COMPRESSED

The Burping Bag

Once the chemicals have split apart, each chemical is free to react with other chemicals, like the sodium bicarbonate powder. The chloride reacts with the sodium in the sodium bicarbonate to form table salt and carbon dioxide, which is a gas. A gas takes up considerably more space than a liquid, and this extra gas causes the bag to swell.

As the amount of gas inside the bag increases, the pressure inside the bag also increases. All of this gas pressure puts considerable strain on the plastic lock that is holding everything inside. When the pressure gets to be too much, the zip lock gives, and the gas rushes out rapidly. This creates a pressure wave, or giant vibration, that our ears perceive as a "boom."

Science Fair Extensions

13. Experiment with different sizes of bags and see if the amount of air inside the bag makes a difference in the boom that is created.

14 Design some equipment that uses this chemical reaction to produce the sound made by a whoopie cushion, rather than an explosion.

15. Compare this chemical reaction with the chemical reaction that a firecracker undergoes when it explodes. List the similarities and differences between both reactions.

Big Idea 3

Sound is a form of energy and can be converted to or from other sources of energy.

Soup Can Oscilloscope

The Experiment

An oscilloscope shows sound in a visual way so that it can be studied. As you construct and use this oscilloscope, or "Laser Reflector Apparatus," you will enjoy producing your sound waves to convey observations and newly-found knowledge to one another. In other words, you get to yap.

This experiment will have you *seeing* sound. This is a takeoff on a real piece of sound technology called an oscilloscope. For our purposes, let's call what you produce a "Photon Reflector Apparatus," or PRA for short. It will allow you to see our sound vibrations in a manner that resembles a light show. Once you have experienced this, you will want to do your own investigative work on the side, using your PRA at home. In the meantime, let's go *looking* for sound waves.

Materials

1   #303 soup can, empty, and clean, both ends removed
1   Mirror square, 1" by 1",
    or seeral sequins
1   Balloon, 9" diameter
1   Jar of rubber cement
1   Mini Mag Lite
1   Index card
1   Hole punch
1   Roll of masking tape

Procedure

1. Cut the mouth off the balloon, and stretch the balloon over one of the open ends of the soup can. The other end should be left uncovered.

2. Take the piece of mirror and position it between the middle and the edge of the balloon. Secure it with rubber cement. (You may use sequins instead of the piece of mirror.) You now have a "Photon Reflector Apparatus."

3. Punch a hole in the center of the index card, and then tape the card over the light-emitting end of a flashlight. Use the illustration at the right as a guide.

4. Place the light source on a flat table. Carefully hold the soup can over your mouth and sit so that the light is shining directly on the mirror or sequins. There is a picture of this set-up on the next page.

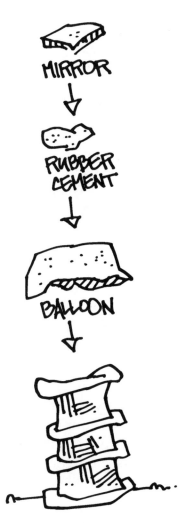

5. Ask a friend to locate the reflected light dots on the wall Place your mouth over the open end of the can and, while watching the reflected laser light on the wall, talk, yell, or carry on in a vocal manner into the can. The person looking at the reflected light should see it bounce and dance around as you produce sound.

6. Try to make a variety of sounds at different levels of volume and pitch.

Soup Can Oscilloscope

7. Form a variety of words or sounds, like the vowel sounds we all practiced in first grade. Try having two or more "light shows" going on next to one another while making the same sounds. Do the "light shows" match? Are they similar in any way?

How Come, Huh?

When you spoke into the open end of the can, sound waves traveled from your mouth to the rubber surface of the balloon. When they hit the rubber surface, they bounced off it, causing it to move. In the process, you converted sound energy to physical energy (the moving of the rubber surface.)

Science Fair Extensions

16. Research real oscilloscopes. What are they used for? Try to get someone to bring one in and demonstrate it.

17. Make a giant version of this wave reflector using a gallon can, a piece of rubber dam from a dentist's office, and a handful of sequins. Place the can in front of a stereo speaker that you crank up. If you have a bright light trained on the can, you will see a disco effect as the reflected beams of light dance all over the room.

Squealing Balloon

The Experiment

Sound and vibration ... a number of activities come to mind, but first and foremost ... the infamous whoopie cushion and squealing balloon ideas—When air is trapped in a flexible container, which both a whoopie cushion and balloon are, the air is anxious to get out. When the restraint that holds the opening closed is allowed or forced to open, the air rushes out, causing the rubber at the opening to vibrate. If the vibrations are slow, we have a low, resonant Bronx Cheer. If the vibrations are quick and fast, we have an annoying, high-pitched squeal. The upshot of this experiment is that we can use mechanical energy and air pressure to create sound.

Materials

1   Balloon
1   Set of lungs
1   Whoopie cushion

Procedure

1. Blow the balloon up about halfway. Use your thumb and index finger on either side of the opening to prevent the air from escaping from the balloon. When you are ready, release your hold on the opening and let the air rush out as fast as it possibly can.

2. Return the balloon to its previous blown-up state and release the air again, but this time hold the opening of the balloon very tightly and allow only a small amount of air to escape. Compare the pitch of the second balloon to the pitch of the first.

Squealing Balloon

3. Next, inflate a whoopie cushion and sit on it. Repeat this a few times. Compare the pitches created by the vibrations and speculate about the speed and tautness of the rubber at the opening.

How Come, Huh?

Hmmm! Why, why, why? As human beings, we are always questioning things. Why did that whoopie cushion sound so good back when Mrs. Thompson sat on it in 3rd grade, but not in Mr. Bieber's 6th-grade science class when he sat down to grade our tests?

As the air from the balloon slipped past the opening of the rubbery material, the air pushed on the rubber and caused it to vibrate back and forth rapidly. This rapid back-and-forth movement, or vibration, caused a sound to be produced. Just like your vocal cords, as the material that is vibrating stretches, the pitch becomes higher. As it loosens, it lowers.

With the whoopie cushion, it is the same idea. Air is trapped inside a large container. You plop your fanny on the container, putting even more pressure on the air, and forcing some of it out. The air rushes out of the opening, pushes on the rubber, and gets it to vibrate. The vibrating rubber causes the air to vibrate and produces the enticing sound that we all know and love.

Science Fair Extensions

18. The balloon activity showed you how variation in pitch is caused by changing the elasticity of the opening to the balloon. Use your balloon to play a sliding scale. Let a continuous stream of air out of the balloon, and slowly release the tension on the balloon's neck. Then stretch the balloon to create more tension, enabling you to play a musical scale or a simple tune.

19. Have some brass instrument players from the band come and demonstrate how they produce the sound that comes from their instruments. Look at the sizes of mouthpieces from trumpet to tuba. What might the sizes of the mouthpieces have to do with the sounds these instruments produce?

20. Get a set of Scottish bagpipes and see how they work. They are a masterpiece of sound engineering!

Pouring Sound

The Experiment

With a propane torch, you are going to heat a folded piece of metal-alloy screen, stuffed into one end of a large-diameter steel tube. When the torch is removed, the tube begins to hum. If you tilt the tube sideways, giving the illusion that you are "pouring" the sound out of the tube, the sound will stop. If you quickly turn the tube so that it's in a vertical position, the sound will resume.

In addition to creating a wonderful trick for the kids, you are also using heat to create a convection current that rises and vibrates in the tube. This produces sound. (Sure enough, this is another example of converting energy.)

Materials

1 Propane torch
   or Bunsen burner
1 Propane torch stand
1 Ignitor or book of matches
1 Oven mitt
1 Steel tube, 19" by 1.5"
1 Metal-alloy screen, 2" by 6"
1 Hammer
1 Large, opaque, plastic cup
1 Pair of goggles
1 Wooden dowel
   or Screwdriver
Adult supervision

Procedure

1. These tubes are easy and relatively inexpensive to make. Head to the plumbing or hardware section of your local home improvement store, and explain you are a science enthusiast. Describe the experiment.

The pipe is a section of the fence-post that holds up a metal fence. The screen is a 20-gauge metal alloy that can be cut into a 2 by 6 strip, tri-folded into a 2" by 2" square, and then pounded into the bottom of the pipe using a wooden dowel and hammer.

2. With your goggles on and with an adult by your side, fire up the torch and put the oven mitt on the hand in which you'll hold the tube.

3. The key to this experiment is to get the screen inside the bottom of the tube red hot using the torch. To achieve this, you are going to want to hold the tube upright, with the metal-alloy screen toward the end that is nearest the torch. Use the illustration to the left as a guide.

4. Insert the flame of the torch into the bottom of the tube, so that it heats the alloy screen directly. When the screen gets hot enough, the tube will begin to hum, *but not until you remove the flame from inside the tube*. This usually takes about 15 to 20 seconds. Every tube is different, so it would be a good idea to practice and time your particular tube before you uncork this one for your friends.

Pouring Sound

5. When the screen is hot enough, the tube starts to hum, eyeballs bug out, and your friends are really impressed. Don't stop now; it's zinger time. Pick up the large, opaque, plastic cup. Hold the cup up, and tilt the tube at an angle, so that it looks like you are literally "pouring" the sound from the tube into the cup. The interesting thing is that, as soon as you tip the tube over, the sound ceases.

6. Quickly return the tube to its upright position and "pour" the sound back into the tube from the cup. It will start to hum again. Depending on how hot you got the screen, you may be able to "pour" the sound back and forth several times before the screen cools to the point where it will not produce the convection current necessary to produce the sound. As with comedy, omelettes, and good science demos, timing is everything.

How Come, Huh?

Touch a lit propane torch to anything, and it's a sure bet that it is going to get hot. As the hot screen heats the air inside the tube, a convection current starts to form, and the air rises through the tube. The air escaping from the top of the tube creates an area of low pressure, just above the screen, and cold air enters the bottom of the tube. As it passes through the hot screen, it is heated rapidly and starts to rise turbulently through the tube. This turbulent motion produces a wave of vibrating air molecules that our ears interpret as a "hum."

When you tip the tube sideways, you disrupt the movement of the air. Because air molecules don't get a chance to bounce around inside the tube and produce the vibrations, the sound ceases. By returning the tube to its vertical position, the air is free to rise and produce sound again. For the record, you cannot pour sound. It's an illusion— that is, if it is well done. That's where the practice comes in.

Science Fair Extensions

21. Make a set of pipes of different lengths and diameters. Again, the home improvement store will have a variety of different pipes, made out of different materials. Determine how these two variables, length and diameter, affect the pitch that is produced.

22. Find out if the local church has a set of organ pipes— same concept, slightly more refined. Create an experiment that allows you to replicate a church organ pipe.

23. Propane torches throw out a lot of heat and produce a very chaotic, violent column of air. That is why you have to remove the torch before the sound becomes audible.

It is possible to produce the same kind of effect and a much more gentle tone using candles and tubes. Experiment, with the permission of your parents, and see if you can come up with a new musical instrument.

24. Combine this experiment with a convection current fan to demonstrate the presence and location of hot air rising out of the tube.

Amp It Up

The Experiment

You've produced sound from different sources of energy. This time you'll use electicity and a simple buzzer to produce the sound. The trick to this buzzer is that it works only when electricity is flowing through it in the proper direction. You'll have to figure out what the proper direction is. Then once you are able to produce the annoying buzz that is characteristic of this instrument, we will introduce you to the Morse Code.

Materials

1   Switch
3   Alligator clips
1   Buzzer
1   Battery with battery clip

Procedure

1. Using a battery, 2 alligator clips, and the buzzer, build the simple circuit that is pictured below. As you connect the buzzer to the battery, one of two things will happen. You will either hear an annoying buzz, or you will be greeted by silence. If you hear the buzz, hooray! Note which wire, red or black, is connected to the negative side of the battery.

A. Red
B. Black

A	. -
B	- . . .
C	- . - .
D	- . .
E	.
F	. . - .
G	- - .
H	. . . .
I	. .
J	. - - -
K	- . -
L	. - . .
M	- -
N	- .
O	- - -
P	. - - .
Q	- - . -
R	. - .
S	. . .
T	-
U	. . -
V	. . . -
W	. - -
X	- . . -
Y	- . - -
Z	- - . .

2. Just to make sure this is a one-way buzzer, reverse the wires and see if you can produce any sound.

3. Finally, build the second circuit, pictured at the top of this page, and use your switch to buzz your counterparts in Morse Code. Morse Code is displayed at the right-hand side of this page.

How Come, Huh?

The electricity causes a thin membrane, just like a kazoo, to vibrate back and forth. The membrane vibrates, or pushes against the air, and causes sound to be produced.

Using Morse Code, which was created by Samuel Morse, write a simple message to your friend. Then use your buzzer to transmit it. Ask your friends to write down the letters they think you are trying to send. Compare the message you sent with the message they received. If you have time, switch roles.

0	- - - - -
1	. - - - -
2	. . - - -
3	. . . - -
4	. . . . -
5	. . . . .
6	- . . . .
7	- - . . .
8	- - - . .
9	- - - - .

Amp It Up

Message You Wish to Send:_____
_____.

Letter Sent	Morse Code Sent	Morse Code Received	Letter Rec'd
____	_____	_____	____
____	_____	_____	____
____	_____	_____	____
____	_____	_____	____
____	_____	_____	____
____	_____	_____	____
____	_____	_____	____
____	_____	_____	____
____	_____	_____	____
____	_____	_____	____
____	_____	_____	____
____	_____	_____	____
____	_____	_____	____
____	_____	_____	____
____	_____	_____	____

Science Fair Extensions

25. Research decibels, deafness, and how they correlate.

26. With your parents' permission, take apart a speaker and try to figure out its parts and what makes it tick.

Big Idea 4

Sound travels as one of two kinds of waves—compression and transverse. The parts of these waves can be identified as the crest, trough, amplitude, node, and antinode.

Jump Rope Waves

The Experiment

It is very hard to see sound and light waves, but we can see their effects on things like puffed rice, soap films, and reflections off mirrors and sequins. To understand how these kinds of waves travel and what they look like, we are going to use a jump rope in this lab and a metal spring in the next.

First up is a transverse wave, which is a wave that moves in one direction as the particles of the medium move across the wave. In other words, this type of wave will move from one end of the rope to the other, but also up and down at the same time. Grab a rope from an elementary school kid and let's see what we are talking about.

Materials

1   Rope
1   Doorknob
    Energy from an arm

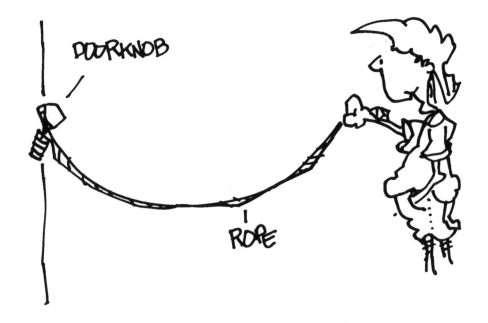

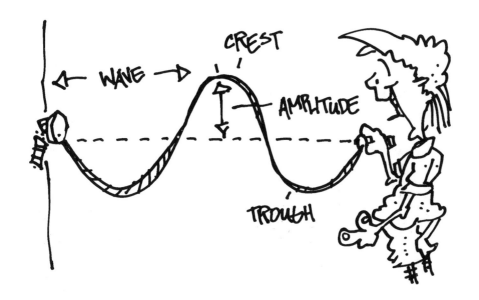

Procedure

1. Tie one end of a jump rope to a doorknob, using the illustration on the bottom of the previous page as a guide.

2. Hold on to the other end of the jump rope and back away from the doorknob until most of the slack has been taken out of the rope. The rope will form a shallow "U". Again, the illustration on the previous page will help.

3. Quickly lift the end of the rope up and down once and observe the wave that travels to the doorknob. This is a transverse wave. The energy traveled down the rope lengthwise, but the particles (the rope) moved in a perpindicular motion, up and down.

4. You are going to create what is called a standing wave. Take the end of the rope and move it up and down quickly until you get a permanent wave forming. The other name for this is a standing wave. A standing wave will allow you to see the trough (bottom), crest (top), node (center), and amplitude (height) of the wave.

Jump Rope Waves

5. Speed up the motion of your hand and, rather than creating a one-wave standing wave, go fast enough to create a two-wave standing wave. This will allow you to see all the features of the previous wave, along with a new one, the antinode.

6. Finally, if your rope is long enough and your hands are quick enough, see if you can get three standing waves to appear on your rope.

7. Go back to making a single standing wave. Holding the rope in one hand and shortening it with your other, move closer to the doorknob. Describe the amplitude of the wave, as well as the length of the wave. _____

_____

_____

8.   Back away from the doorknob. Describe the amplitude of the wave and length of the wave now. _____

_____

_____

9.   Move your hand back and forth instead of up and down. Repeat all of the experiments that you were instructed to perform for this lab. Do the waves work just as well when they are sideways as when they are vertical?

How Come, Huh?

As you move your hand up and down, you are sending energy from one end of the rope to the other. The rope moves in a snake-like pattern. The highest point of the wave on the rope is the crest, and the lowest is the trough. If you drew an imaginary line from your hand to the doorknob, the amplitude would be the distance from that line to the crest of the wave, or the distance from the imaginary line to the trough.   If this were a sound wave, the higher the amplitude, the louder the sound would be to your ears.

If you were to measure the length of the wave from node to node, you would find the frequency of the wave. The shorter the wave, the higher the frequency and the higher the pitch the object would be making. If the waves are long and the frequency is long, the pitch would be low.

Science Fair Extension

27. Use other kinds of materials to create your standing waves. See if some work better than others.

Slinky Wars

The Experiment

You and a friend will use a metal Slinky to send waves of energy back and forth. You will vary the strength of the energy by holding different numbers of coils and pushing the Slinky with varying degrees of force. Sound moves in both compression and transverse waves. The Slinky makes a good model for both kinds of sound waves. This is a great visual example of energy being transferred through matter while the matter remains in place. Beware the tangled Slinky mess!

You and your friend will stand at each end of a table and spread a Slinky between you. Each of you will keep a firm hold on one end of the Slinky, which will remain touching the table. To create a compression wave, one of you will gather up about 20 coils and then release them so that they will travel as a clump down the spring toward your partner. Transverse waves up next ... !

Materials

1 Slinky
1 Table, the longer the better
1 Partner

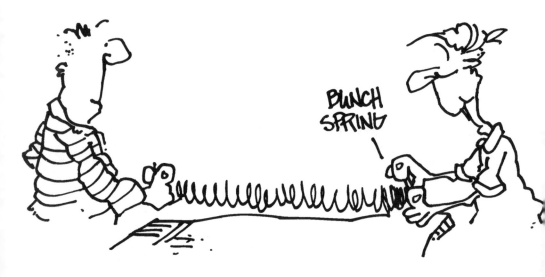

BUNCH SPRING

Procedure

1. One student stands at each end of the table and holds an end of the Slinky in one hand.

2. First up are the compression waves. Take turns gathering a few coils of the Slinky and releasing them down the table to your partner's end. **Do not** release your end of the spring when you let go of the coil you made.

3. Observe how the energy wave moves and how, once it arrives at the end of the spring, it is reflected back to you. Vary the number of coils held and released and observe the movement.

WAVE

TOP VIEW

STANDING WAVE

Slinky Wars

4. Once you have perfected compression waves, it is time for the transverse wave experiments. First up, you'll look at reflected waves. Send a wave down to your partner and note if it is on your left or right. When the wave gets to your partner, it will be reflected back to you. Is it on the same side or on the opposite side?

5. Next, you want to set up a standing wave. To do this, you will keep moving the spring back and forth until you have a "permanent" wave on your table. Use the diagram on the previous page.

How Come, Huh?

When you gather the springs together, you are adding energy to them. As they are released, the springs coil forward, and each spring compresses the ones in front of it. The result is called a compression wave, which you can now say that you have seen personally.

The transverse wave was the second wave you produced. This is more typical of what folks think of when they think about waves. These waves have a crest, trough, period, and node.

Science Fair Extensions

28. You created a standing transverse wave. Now, see if you can figure out a way to create a standing compression wave.

29. Put the Slinky in a freezer and introduce the variable of temperature to your test. Does the temperature of the spring affect this experiment in any way?

30. Change the table surface by covering it with cardboard or wax paper. See how this affects the speed and size of the waves that travel down the spring. Be sure to test both transverse and compression waves.

Super Snuffer

The Experiment

Air ... We can't live without it, and we can't see it, but we can "see" it is there by sending things through it. Confused yet ... ? There's more. We need air, and if we don't respire, we expire. This is definitely a case of cause and effect, if there ever was one. By creating and using an air cannon, you can experiment with the movement of air. We'll be looking at what are known as compression waves.

In this lab we are going to convert an ordinary, old, empty, unloved, oatmeal container into a semi-high-tech pneumatic blaster that can knock down paper dummies and extinguish candle flames from a distance of up to five feet. Cool.

Materials

1   Oatmeal container, empty
1   Pair of scissors
1   Pencil
1   Dime
1   Metric ruler
    and
1   Book of matches
1   Votive candle
    or
1   Paper target
    Adult supervision

Procedure

1. Remove the lid from your container and make sure that all of the contents have been removed. (Dump any leftover oatmeal into the garbage can.)

Super Snuffer

2. Place the container upside down on the table. Put the dime in the center of the container and trace around it, using the pencil. Set the dime aside.

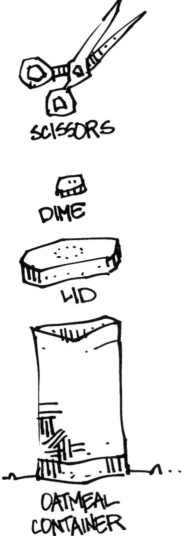

SCISSORS

DIME

LID

OATMEAL CONTAINER

3. Using the point of one of the scissor blades, gently insert the scissors into the cardboard and make a small hole in the center of the circle that you made when you traced around the dime. Once the blade is inside the container, snip a small hole, following the outline of the dime as a guide.

4. Replace the cardboard lid on the top of the container. The lid is now known as the "thumping zone." When you are asked to hit it, tap it directly in the center by releasing your center finger from behind your thumb. If it helps, make an X in the center of the lid. Your super snuffer is now ready.

5. Place your super snuffer on the table and mark the opening with a small piece of masking tape. Place the candle or the target found on page 67, 15 centimeters from the edge of the tape. Aim the opening at the target. Holding the top of the container with one hand, give the thumping zone a tap by flicking it with your center finger.

6. If the flame was extinguished or your target tipped over, place an *X* in the *15 centimeter* column. Fire your cannon at the target three times, from each distance. Record your observations each time. If you hit the target two out of three times, then mark the boxes under the distances from which you did it. Move the target back 5 centimeters and shoot again. If you are having trouble visualizing this, there is an illustration right above that should help. Repeat this until you can no longer extinguish the flame or tip the target over.

Data & Observations

Experiment with knocking over the target, found on page 67, or extinguishing the candle flame. Note the distances from which your cannon hit its target by marking an *X* in the appropriate columns in the data table below.

Distance	15cm	20cm	25cm	30cm	35cm	40cm
Trial 1						
Trial 2						
Trial 3						

Super Snuffer

How Come, Huh?

As the "thumping zone" was struck, the air molecules inside the container were compressed or pushed together. Just as when you squeeze a balloon that is full of air, the air must search for a place to go. In this case, the air found a hole through which to escape. This caused the air to come rushing out with great energy, focused in a narrow wave that traveled at high speed. When this wave of air encounted the target, it blew it over; when it came in contact with the candle flame, the flame was extinguished.

Science Fair Extensions

31. Vary the hole size in the Super Snuffer to see if it has any effect on the kind of air wave that is sent out.

32. Vary the type and thickness of material that you use to make the "thumping zone." Rubbery types of materials work well, but try others, such as plastic or cardboard. Let your imagination run wild.

33. Make an extra super snuffer using a 5-gallon bucket, small garbage can, or other container. Cut a hole in one end of the super snuffer and set your target up at the other end of the garage. Have fun and experiment with different materials for the thumping zone, as well as different sizes for the hole at the front of the snuffer.

Super Snuffer Target

Fold on dotted line to make a stand for the target.

Singing Rods

The Experiment

You will be able to create a dissonant and quite annoying demonstration of how compression waves can be amplified in a metal rod, simply by stroking the rod with your fingers and a little pine sap (rosin) to set up a standing wave. This is guaranteed to annoy all the dogs and most of the cats for a couple of miles.

Materials

3   Aluminum rods
1   Baggie of rosin
1   Set of fingers
    Ear plugs (optional)

Procedure

1. Dip your thumb and forefinger into the rosin to get a light dusting on them. Coat one-half of the rod with the rosin by rubbing your fingers back and forth on the rod. (It helps if you sprinkle some extra rosin on the top half of the rod and then spread it out with your fingers.)

2. Hold the rod right in the middle with your left hand, two fingers on top and thumb on the bottom. Take the thumb and forefinger of your right hand and "wipe" the rosin off the rod by moving your fingers down the rod, applying a fair amount of pressure while moving at a pretty good clip.

3. When you get to the end of the rod, remove your fingers and quickly bring them back to the middle of the rod. Rub again. At first, it may take 15 to 20 seconds to get the rod to sing. Once you practice, you can achieve an ear-splitting pitch in two or three wipes.

The trick is to set up a standing wave. As you practice, this will get easier and easier.

How Come, Huh?

The rosin is sticky; it's pine sap. The friction that is produced between your fingers and the rod caused the metal to form a compression wave that traveled from end to end at a very high speed. Because the rod was cut to a perfect length, the waves almost immediately began bouncing from middle to end, multiplying the effect that you heard in the form of a standing wave.

Science Fair Extensions

34. As you make the ringing sound with your rod, place one end of the vibrating rod in a bowl or bucket of water. Watch the results. You should be able to see the vibrations as the sound waves are transferred from the rod to the water.

35. Try using rods of different lengths to produce different sounds. When we demonstrate this lab activity, we use rods that are cut to 24", 30", and 36", which all produce dramatic results.

Big Idea 5

Pitch can be varied by changing the rate of vibration. The rate of vibration can be varied by changing the length or thickness of the vibrating object. The faster an object vibrates, the higher the pitch it produces.

Bottle Band

The Experiment

Strike up the band! In this activity, you will vary the amount of water in glass bottles to produce a variety of sounds. (You know the score, right … ? The longer the instrument, the lower the pitch …)

Materials

7   Glass bottles, 12-16 oz.
1   Roll of masking tape
1   Felt marker
1   Spoon
1   Set of lips and lungs
    Water

Procedure

1. Line up all 7 of the bottles. Put a small piece of tape on each of the bottles. Number the pieces of tape, 1 through 7, with a felt marker.

2. Starting with Bottle 1, which you will leave empty, gradually fill each bottle with a little more water than you used to fill the previous one. Keep filling until you reach Bottle 7, which you should fill to within an inch of its top. (Use the illustration shown here as a guide.)

Bottle Band

3. Using your spoon, tap the middle of Bottle 1. Listen to the pitch that is produced. Then tap Bottle 7 and compare its pitch to that of Bottle 1. Is the pitch produced higher or lower? Circle your answer below.

A. Higher
B. Lower

4. Tap each of the bottles with the spoon and determine how the amount of water in a bottle affects the pitch that is produced. Write your answer in the observation section on the next page.

5. You are now going to create a sound by placing your lower lip against the edge of the bottle top and blowing across the top of the bottle. Some of the air will enter the bottle, bounce off the water and vibrate back up out the top, producing a sound. Give this a try.

6. After you have mastered producing a sound, blow into each of the bottles. Arrange them from lowest- to highest-pitch. Then try to play a scale and a tune with your "bottle band."

Data and Observations

1. The order of bottles, from lowest-to highest-pitch, when tapping the side of each bottle with a spoon is as follows:

— — — — — — —

2. The order of bottles, from lowest-to highest-pitch, when blowing across the top of each bottle is as follows:

— — — — — — —

How Come, Huh?

You should have observed two different reactions. When tapping the glass with the spoon, the bottle with the most water in it should have had the lowest pitch. The reason for this is that the vibration producing the sound is vibrating through the water. The more water there is, the lower the pitch will be.

When you blew across the bottle, you were causing the column of air to vibrate. The longer the column of air that is inside the bottle, the lower the pitch will be.

Science Fair Extension

36. Demonstrate that bottle shape affects the pitch that is produced when you blow across the top of a bottle.

Kamakazie Straw Flute

The Experiment

You will need one naked straw for this experiment. Once in the buff, the straw is cut, following the pattern on this page, and flattened, using a pair of scissors. Place the straw inside your mouth, just behind your lips, so that each end is free to vibrate. When a large volume of air is pushed through the straw rapidly, it causes the cut plastic to vibrate, producing an obnoxious buzzing sound. Who needs fingernails on a chalkboard?

Materials

1   Straw
1   Pair of scissors
1   Pair of lungs

Procedure

1. We are going to start with the skinny straw. Cut the top of the straw into the shape that is pictured at the right.

2. Once it is cut, flatten the end with a pair of scissors or your thumb. If it is a plastic straw (as opposed to paper), it may take several good, hard rubs to get it flat. Snip two small triangles from the end of the straw to produce the shape that you see here.

3. Wet the cut end of the straw with

CUTS

your mouth and, with the straw inside your mouth and past your lips an inch or so, blow into the straw as hard as you can. The cut ends should vibrate and produce an obnoxious sound. If you have a difficult time doing this, it may be because you are not using enough air or you need to put more of the straw in your mouth. Blow from your diaphragm (stomach area) and really push.

4.   Once you have the straw flute down pat, take the scissors and, while you are blowing into the straw, cut the straw shorter and shorter, changing the pitch of the straw.

How Come, Huh?

As the air passes over the opening that has been cut, it causes the cut ends of the straw to vibrate. The movement of the plastic compresses the air inside the tube, creating sound waves which come out the other end of the straw. The pitch of the instrument is directly proportional to the length. The longer the instrument, the lower the pitch will be, and vice-versa.

Science Fair Extension

37. Make straw flutes using straws of different diameters. See if the diameter has any effect on the pitch that is produced by the instrument.

s' Trombones

The Experiment

An s' Trombone is a straw trombone. What we are going to do is build on the previous lab. Once you get the straw flute thing going, we are going to show you how to create an instrument that will allow you to alter the pitch or note that you produce without having to cut the plastic.

A cut skinny straw is inserted into the end of a fatter straw. When you start to blow, you slide the fat straw back and forth over the skinny straw. As the length of the instrument changes, the pitch changes, as well.

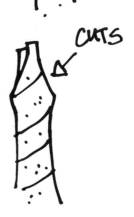

CUTS

Materials

1   Skinny straw
1   Fat straw
1   Pair of scissors
1   Pair of lungs

Procedure

1. We are going to start with the skinny straw again. Cut the top of the straw into the shape that is pictured at the right. This should be old hat if you just tried the previous lab.

If it has been a while since you made straw flutes, or if you skipped the previous lab, you will want to practice getting the straw to work.

2. Once you have the straw flute down pat, insert the fat straw over the skinny straw. Make a trombone-type instrument by sliding the larger straw up and down the tube of the skinny straw while you are blowing.

3. Once you get the hang of playing your straw trombone, you may want to figure out exactly where the notes on your instrument are and mark them with a felt marker.

How Come, Huh?

As the air passes over the opening that has been cut, it causes the cut ends of the straw to vibrate. The movement of the plastic compresses the air inside the tube, creating sound waves which come out the other end of the straw. The pitch of the instrument is directly proportional to the length. The longer the instrument, the lower the pitch will be.

When you added the second straw, you were, in effect, changing the instrument so that you could manipulate its length without having to cut it. When the straw was all the way out, it produced a low pitch. When it was all the way up, it produced a higher pitch.

Science Fair Extension

38. Some convenience stores sell a sour candy powder in a long, thick, plastic straw. Use this straw to make a super s' Trombone that produces very low notes. It's time to wake up all the dogs in the neighborhood.

Water Whistle

The Experiment

This lab utilizes a simple straw that is snipped in just the right way to create a unique whistle. This is a great way to understand how different amounts of air within a space can create different vibrations and sounds. This lab builds on ideas that were presented in the bottle band activity.

Materials

1   Straw, plastic
1   Metric ruler
1   Cup of water
1   Set of lungs, full of air
1   Pair of scissors

Procedure

1. Measure down from the top of your straw about 5 centimeters and snip into the side of the straw. Do not snip all the way through.

2. Cut carefully through the straw, but leave a tiny piece to connect the top section of the straw to the bottom section.

3. Bend the top of the straw so that it forms a right angle with the bottom. Use the illustration at the right as a guide.

CUT HERE

LEAVE ATTACHED

4. Place the long, fat end of the straw in a cup of water and blow into the skinny top section of the straw. What you should hear is a whistle as the air moves across the larger straw and bounces off the water.

5. Lower the straw into the water as you blow. Did the pitch get higher or lower?

6. Raise and lower the straw so that a fine mist sprays from the bottom section as you blow across the opening and observe the position of the straw.

How Come, Huh?

When you blow across the top of the straw, you are caus-ing the air to vibrate in the bot-tom length of the straw. These vibrations create sound waves. As you raise the straw, a greater amount of air is in the bottom section of the straw, and the pitch becomes lower. When you raise the cup, the section of air in the straw is smaller, and the pitch becomes higher. This is just like the bottle band.

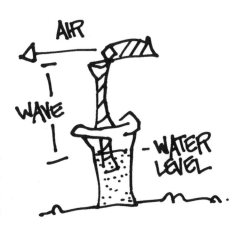

Science Fair Extensions

39. This is messy but fun! Position the straws at a right angle and blow until you cause a fine mist to spew from the bottom section of the straw. You have created a low pressure area that forces the air in the cup out through the straw.

40. Try using different-sized straws and tubes for a variety of pitches.

PVC Orchestra

The Experiment

In the previous four experiments, you forced air into tubes, causing it to bounce and vibrate and produce a sound. In this experiment you are going to shove air through a tube, using the palm of your hand.

When you whack one end of an open tube against the palm of your hand, you force a column of air up through the tube. Depending on the length of the tube, you get a variety of pitches. Your job is to not only be able to produce the sound, but to determine, mathematically, what length each tube should be cut into.

Materials

1   Pair of scissors
1   5' length of $1/_2$" PVC pipe
1   Metric ruler

Procedure

1. Measure and cut a section of PVC pipe that is 20-cm long.

2. Hold your palm upright and, grasping the pipe in your other hand, bring it straight down onto your palm, as if you were trying to impale yourself. When you hit the fleshy part of your hand, you should almost immediately hear a sound.

3. Continue to build your orchestra by cutting pipe in same-sized increments … say, 3 cm or so. When you cut your second pipe, whap it on the palm of your hand and listen for the tone that is produced. Compare it with the first tone.

4. Cut a third pipe that is shorter than the original. Whap it on your hand. You are going to want to listen, record the measurements, and try your best to determine how much to cut for each different note. The goal is that, when you are done building your orchestra, you are going to have a whole scale to play a song with.

How Come, Huh?

When you whap the tube against the palm of your hand, air is compressed rapidly up into the tube. This compressed air rushes up the tube and pushes against the air inside the tube. This, in turn, causes the air to vibrate, and a sound is produced. The longer the tube and the longer the wavelength, the lower the pitch of the sound will be. The shorter the tube and the shorter the wavelength, the higher the sound will be.

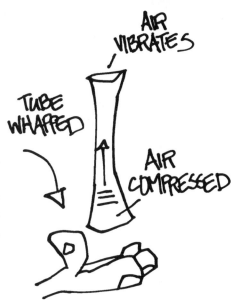

Science Fair Extensions

41. The diameter of the tube definitely has an effect on the pitch that is produced. Design an experiment that proves this particular idea.

42. Compare tubes made from paper or cardboard to those made from plastic. Do they produce similar or different sounds? This is another experiment for the curious and inventive to pursue.

Desktop Vibrations

The Experiment

Every kid who has made it to at least the second grade has, at one time or another, taken a ruler, held it over the edge of a desk, and given it a good whack. The resulting vibrations produced a rather funny noise that can be modified if the length of the ruler is also modified. Anarchy ... ? The crossroads to societal nuisance, or simply a curious, scientific mind at work on one of many of life's pleasant little discoveries ... ? We vote for the latter. Rulers up!

Materials

1   Desk
1   Pair of hands
1   Metric ruler

Procedure

1. Hold the ruler over the desk at the 20centimeter mark. Press down firmly on the 10 centimeters that are still on the desk and push down on the 20 centimeters that extends over the desk. Let go. You will see the ruler vibrating up and down very rapidly and will hear a funny sound.

2. Move the ruler to the 15cm mark and give it another whack. The portion of the ruler that is able to vibrate is shorter this time. Is the pitch of the sound higher or lower? Circle your answer.

A. Higher
B. Lower

3. Try the ruler at the following lengths—5cm, 10cm, 15cm, 20cm, and 25cm. Listen to the pitch of the sound that is produced and place the lengths in order, from highest- to lowest-pitch. The order, from highest to lowest is _____, _____, _____, _____, and _____.

4. Place the ruler at the 25cm mark, only 5cm on the desk and the rest, hanging over. Start the ruler vibrating with a good, hard, whack and then, while the ruler is still vibrating, slide the ruler back over the table, making the portion that is extended over the end shorter and shorter.

How Come, Huh?

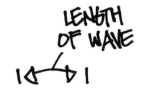

The portion of the ruler that was allowed to vibrate determined the pitch of the sound. When there was a lot of wood or plastic hanging over the edge of the desk, then a low pitch was produced. When the vibrating part was shorter, the pitch was higher.

Science Fair Extension

43. You can make an instrument called a popsicle piano. Actually, you use tongue depressors and a block of wood. Position the tongue depressors over the edge of the wood block and hold them in place with staples or tacks. As you twang the tongue depressors, they produce sounds of different pitches.

Tissue Box Guitar

The Experiment

Ever want to form your own band? Well this probably isn't the way to do it, but you will have fun trying as you learn about the different sounds or pitches you can get from just one rubber band. Why stop at one rubber band though? Make a rubber band guitar with multiple bands, and let the creativity flow.

The last several labs have focused on the movement of air in closed containers. This lab demonstrates how vibrating objects produce sound, and how that sound is changed by the length and thickness of the vibrating object.

Materials

4   Rubber bands
    (differing lengths and thicknesses)
1   Tissue box, empty
2   Pencils
1   Pair of scissors

Procedure

1. Choose a set of rubber bands of varying thicknesses and stretch them around the box. There should be enough space between them to pluck one without interfering with the others.

2. Slide a pencil under the four rubber bands so that they are lifted off the surface of the tissue box. Use the illustration at the right as a guide.

BANDS

PENCIL

TISSUE BOX

3. Pluck each of the rubber bands and listen to the pitch that it produces. Below, rank the rubber bands from highest pitch (1) to lowest (4).

A. Thinnest _____
B. Thin _____
C. Thicker _____
D. Thickest _____

How Come, Huh?

The thicker the rubber band, the longer the vibration or sound wave it will carry. This, in turn, makes a lower pitched sound. As the rubber bands become lengthened or thinner, the pitch rises. The vibration becomes quicker, or the wave length becomes shorter, and this causes the pitch to become higher.

Science Fair Extensions

44. Use a piece of wood and some nails to stretch the rubber bands. The rubber bands should all be of the same thickness. The variable that you will change is the amount that the rubber band is stretched.

45. Make an old-time bass out of a wash tub, broom handle, and guitar string (from your local music store). Stretch the string from the top of the handle down to the center of the wash tub. While plucking the string, pull back on the broom handle to change the tension on the string. The more tension, the higher the pitch will be. Then, get ready for the Grand Ol' Opry.

Heavy Tunes

The Experiment

This is the next-to-the-last lab activity in this section, and it allows you to explore how the tension on a piece of string affects the pitch that that string produces. If you've heard the expressions, "high strung" or "strung too tight" and weren't too sure where they came from, you will have a better idea after this lab.

Materials

1   Cotton string, 60" length
1   Thumbtack
1   Piece of wood, 2" by 4" by 4'
1   Table
1   Toy bucket
1   Pencil
1   Toy shovel or large spoon
1   Pile of sand, 2 lbs.
1   Hammer

Procedure

1. Shove a thumbtack into the end of the board, and wrap one end of the string around its base. Hammer the thumbtack the rest of the way into the board.

2. Hang the string over the end of the board and place a pencil under the string. Tie a small toy bucket to the end of the string. Use the illustration on the next page as a guide.

3. The weight of the bucket should pull the string taut. Pluck the string and listen to the sound that is produced. Add a half-pound of sand to the bucket and pluck the string again. Compare the pitch that is produced when the bucket is empty with when it has sand in it. Is it higher or lower?

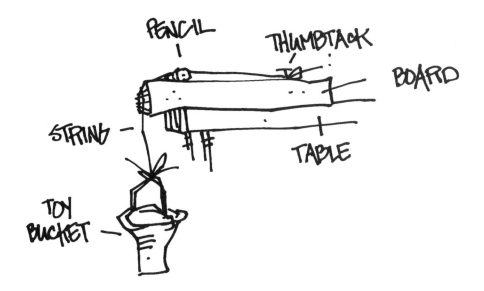

4. Continue to add sand, a half-pound at a time, to the toy bucket. Compare the sound that is produced each time.

How Come, Huh?

As the string becomes more and more taut, it vibrates faster and faster. The faster the string vibrates, the higher the pitch will be. The more weight that you add, the higher the pitch will sound.

Science Fair Extensions

46. Substitute different kinds of material for the string. Try fishing wire, a guitar string, thin copper wire, and anything else that you can find around the house. Compare the quality of the tone as well as the change in pitch as weight is added to the bucket.

47. Find a correlation between the amount of weight added and the note that is produced by the string. Is it a straight mathematical change or is it more exponential?

Portable Rain Shower

The Experiment

And for this lab, we've got vibrations and sound produced by falling popcorn kernels that sound like a rainstorm. A tube is peppered with finishing nails and wrapped with tape. A handful of popcorn is dumped inside. When the tube is capped and tipped upside down, the popcorn kernels fall through the nails. The kernels vibrate, the nails vibrate against the cardboard, and this amplifies the noise and creates a portable rain shower—even during drought conditions.

Materials

1   Mailing tube, cardboard, 2" diameter, with end caps
1   Box of nails, #6
1   Hammer
1   Roll of masking
        or Electrical tape

Procedure

1. Place the caps on each end of the cardboard tube to give it more stability. Hammer the nails into the side of the tube. As you insert each nail, rotate the tube 90 degrees and move down one inch. The nails should be just long enough to almost reach the other side of the tube, but they should not pierce the side.

2.   Once you have hammered all of the nails into the tube, remove one of the end caps and pour in a cup of popcorn kernels. Replace the end cap.

3.   Tip the rain stick on end and listen as all of the popcorn kernels drop and bounce off the nails on their way to the bottom of the tube. When the shower stops, flip the tube over and it will start again.

How Come, Huh?

The center of the tube is partially blocked by the nails. As the popcorn kernels fall through the center of the tube, they hit the nails and begin to vibrate. The nails vibrate against the cardboard, and this amplifies the noise.

Science Fair Extensions

48.   The sound that is produced is a combination of materials and surfaces. In this case, it is metal nails, popcorn kernels, and a cardboard tube. Repeat the experiment and try a large plastic or acrylic tube. You can also replace the popcorn kernels with pebbles or sunflower seeds that are in the shell. Change the variables.

49.   Combine this lab with the Thunder Drum activity to produce a severe weather theater production for your parents, friends, neighbors, and other people who are easily extorted into viewing home theater productions.

Big Idea 6

Sound waves can be transmitted through solids, liquids, and gases, but never through a vacuum.

Sound Baggies

The Experiment

Sound cannot travel through a vacuum, but it can travel through solids, liquids, and gases. This particular lab will give you an opportunity to explore the movement of sound through all three states of matter.

Materials

3   Baggies, resealable
1   Desktop
1   Spoon
1   Ear (attached to brain)
1   Partner
    Sand
    Water
    Air

Procedure

1. Prepare each of the baggies by filling them two-thirds full with sand, water, and air, respectively. Seal each baggie so that the contents remain in the bag.

2. Place the baggies on the desktop.

3. Put your ear flat down on the baggie that is full of sand. Ask your partner to tap the desk with the spoon. Listen for the sound that is produced.

4. Repeat the procedure with the baggie that is full of water, and then with the baggie that is full of sand. Compare the sound that you hear

Sound Baggies

with all three states of matter.

5. When your partner has finished tapping the spoon on the desk, hold the bag of sand up to your ear. Ask your partner to say something to you through the sand. Next, have your partner say something to you through water and then air. Note the sounds that are produced.

Data & Observations

Rank the loudness of the sound of the spoon as it was tapped on the desk and then heard through the baggies. Rank➡1 = loudest; 2 = fairly clear; 3 = least clear.

Solid _____, Liquid _____, Gas _____,

Rank the clarity of the sound of the person talking to you through the baggie of different materials. Rank➡1 = loudest; 2 = fairly clear; 3 = least clear.

Solid _____, Liquid _____, Gas _____,

Rank the density of the three materials that you used. Rank➡1=loudest; 2=fairly clear; 3=least clear.

Solid _____, Liquid _____, Gas _____,

How Come, Huh?

Sound produces longitudinal waves that travel by passing their energy along to the matter that they are traveling through. For example, when we talk, our vocal cords vibrate and push waves out into the air. The waves travel through the air by causing other air molecules to vibrate.

Sound also travels through liquids. Because the molecules of water are much closer together and are prone to bumping into one another, the speed of sound in water is much faster than in air. You can also hear sound over longer distances. Whales have been known to talk to one another at distances of up to 800 miles.

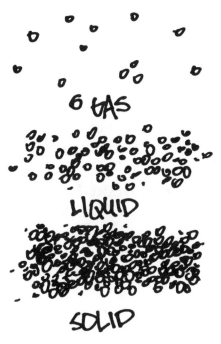

Sound travels fastest in solids. The particles are more dense than those that make up either air or water. Because they are so close together, they pass the sound waves, or energy, quickly from one place to another. Sound traveling through solids can be heard over very long distances and at great speeds.

Science Fair Extension

50. Walk to the far end of a metal fence and place your ear against one of the metal posts that holds the fence upright. Face away from your partner, who will hold a baseball bat or large stick. Ask your partner to whap the fence post. Listen for the sound that travels down the fence to you.

Or, turn the page and do the next activity.

Solid Sound Pathways

The Experiment

This lab will allow you to do two things: demonstrate that sound does, indeed, travel through solids, and take a crude measurement of the speed of sound through metal.

Materials

1   Metal fence
1   Brick wall
1   Concrete sidewalk
1   Asphalt driveway
1   Metal wrench or crowbar
1   Stopwatch
1   Partner
1   Tape measure

Procedure

1. Find a 100-meter section of metal fence. Choose a fencepost to be the starting spot and measure out 100 meters using the tape measure.

2. Ask your partner to stand facing away from you, near the 100-meter mark. Have your partner place an ear against the metal fencepost that is closest to the 100-meter mark and raise a hand.

3. Set your stopwatch to 0. You are going to take the wrench and whack it against the metal fencepost. At the exact same time, you'll start the stopwatch running.

Your partner is going to keep an ear next to the fence. When your partner hears the sound, she will immediately drop her arm.

4. When your partner drops an arm, stop the stopwatch and record the time in seconds in the data table below. Repeat the experiment two more times and find the average amount of time that it takes for sound to travel 100 meters down the fence.

5. Repeat this experiment along a 100-meter brick wall, taking three measurements and recording them in the data table below.

6. Repeat this experiment along a 100-meter section of concrete sidewalk, as well as a 100-meter section of asphalt, taking three measurements each time and recording them in the appropriate sections of the data table below.

Data & Observations

Material	Time 1	Time 2	Time 3	Avg.
Metal Fence				
Brick Wall				
Concrete Sidewalk				
Asphalt Driveway				

Solid Sound Pathways

To calculate the speed of sound, you use the formula:

Speed = Distance ÷ Time

In this case, the distance is 100 meters and the time is the average time, in seconds, that you recorded in your tests. Plug everything into the formulas below and calculate.

Speed (fence)   = 100m ÷ _____ = _____m/s

Speed (brick)   = 100m ÷ _____ = _____m/s

Speed (concrete) = 100m ÷ _____ = _____m/s

Speed (asphalt) = 100m ÷ _____ = _____m/s

How Come, Huh?

Sound moves faster through solids than through liquids and gases. Among solids, the more dense the solid is, the faster the sound moves through that solid. If you were to weigh a sample of each material and calculate its density, you would find that the more dense the material is, the faster the sound would travel through it.

Science Fair Extensions

51. Get different kinds of metal wires and determine the speed that sound traveled down 100 meters of each kind of wire. Compare the speed of sound transmission with the density of the wire.

Soup Can Telephones

The Experiment

OK, in the last experiment we established that sound can pass through solids, liquids, and gases. We are going to take advantage of that knowledge to produce a simple, restricted-access communication device called a soup can telephone. The calling range is negligible, call waiting is nonexistent, but Caller I.D. is virtually guaranteed, and the rates aren't bad either.

Materials

4   #303 soup cans, empty
1   Roll of cotton string
1   Spool of fishing line
1   Hammer
1   Nail
4   Paper clips
1   Roll of masking tape
1   Partner

Procedure

1. Using a nail and hammer, make a small hole in the center of the bottom of two empty soup cans.

2. Push the end of the spool of string through the hole in one of the cans. Be sure to slide it from the bottom of the can to the inside. Tie a paper clip to the end of the string and pull it taut.

PAPER CLIP

STRING

SOUP CAN

Soup Can Telephones

3. Do the same for the other can and connect the loose end of the string in the same way. Use the illustration above as a guide.

4. Now you have two soup can telephones. Pull the string taut and talk to your partner. Have your partner talk to you. Compare the quality of the sound when the string is loose and when it is taut.

5. Make a second set of soup can telephones, this time using fishing line instead of cotton string. Use the cans to talk when the line is taut as well as when the line sags. Compare the quality of the sound. Which provides for a clearer transmission?

6. Add a third line to your telephone company system and see if you can hear two people talking at the same time, or if two people can hear you talking. Experiment with the location of the third line, and how it is attached to the other two.

Data & Observations

1. Talk to your telephone buddy through the cans. One person listens; the other person talks. What happens when the string is pulled tight? _____

2. What happens when the string is loose?_____

_____

3. Can you hook up a 3-way conversation?_____

_____

How Come, Huh?

Sound travels through solids, liquids, and gases. We're focusing on solids, in this case. The sound vibrations were collected by the metal portions of the cans and transferred to the strings. The strings started to vibrate and the sound traveled down a string to a metal can bottom. When the sound waves hit the bottom of the opposite can, they were amplified for your ears.

Science Fair Extensions

52. Try various types of string and see which transmits sound most efficiently.

53. Try all sizes of cans. Compare each can's ability to transmit sound. Also compare the quality of the sound.

54. Try different types of containers—plastic, aluminum, cardboard—and compare the quality of the sound.

Homemade Stethoscope

The Experiment

As Sonny and Cher would have said, "The Beat Goes On!" And if that rock and roll reference doesn't date us, nothing will. This activity confirms that the beat does go on. It uses some creative, inexpensive lab supplies to prove that fact. By adding a piece of plastic tubing to a pair of funnels, you can create a stethoscope that really works.

A stethoscope is an instrument that doctors use to amplify their patients' heartbeats. They use it so that they can not only count the beats, but also listen to the blood entering and leaving the heart and to the valves opening and closing.

You are going to make and use a homemade stethoscope in this lab. Despite the fact that it is a rather crude instrument, you will still be able to hear the beating of your heart and the pumping of your blood. If you shift it to a different location on your body, you will be able to hear the movement of air into and out of your lungs.

Materials

2   12" lengths of rubber tubing, wide
1   12" length of rubber tubing, narrow
1   "T" connector
1   Funnel
1   Heart, beating (Yours should be convenient.)

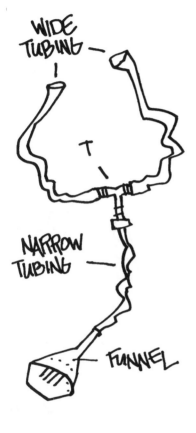

WIDE
TUBING

T

NARROW
TUBING

FUNNEL

Procedure

1. Find the small plastic "T" in your kit. Wiggle the two wide pieces of hose onto either end of the "T". You should have one remaining piece of hose that is narrower than the other two. Place it over the bottom of the "T". Your stethoscope should look like the illustration at the left.

2. Insert the funnel in the loose end of the narrow hose that is hanging down from the "T". Your stethoscope is now complete. A word of caution before you begin: **NEVER SHOUT INTO THE FUNNEL WHILE YOU OR ANYONE ELSE HAS THE TUBES OF THE STETHOSCOPE IN THEIR EARS. YOU COULD CAUSE SERIOUS DAMAGE TO THE EARDRUMS OF THE OFFENDED PARTY.**

3. Carefully insert the two wide tubes into your ears. Place the stethoscope on your chest, a little to the left of your breastbone, and listen for your heartbeat. If the room is quiet, you will not only be able to hear the beating of your heart, but also the opening and closing of your heart valves.

4. Once you find your heartrate and listen to your heart, move the stethoscope around to different areas of your chest and listen to the different sounds that your heart makes. Compare the sound of your heart with those of your classmates; be sure to get permission first.

Homemade Stethoscope

5. After you have exhausted your exploration of the heart, it is time to move on to the lungs. Place the stethoscope in five different places On your chest. Finally, once you have the stethoscope in place, take a deep breath. Listen to the sound of the air rushing into and out of the lungs.

6. Record the number of breaths you take when you are seated and relaxed. Enter that in the data table below.

7. On your teacher's instruction, stand up and do 100 jumping jacks in place. When you are done, sit down and immediately count the number of breaths you take during one minute. Enter this number into the data table.

8. Again, on your teacher's instruction, go outside and run as fast as you can for 3 minutes without stopping. Sit down and immediately take your breathrate for another minute. Enter this number into the data table.

Data & Observations

Activity	Respiration rate/Minute
Sitting	
Jumping Jacks	
Running	

How Come, Huh?

As the valves of the heart open and shut, they produce sound vibrations that travel away from the heart. The cup of your homemade stethoscope acts as a collection device, collecting the sound vibrations from the valves. This sound energy is then channeled into the rubber tubing, where it is directed to your ears via the funnels. The sound enters the ears ... and the rest is sound history.

Science Fair Extensions

55. Study the parts of the heart. Swing by the meat market and ask for a cow's heart. With the permission of your parents, dive into the bovine anatomy.

56. This is a great time to integrate a health unit on exercise and diet. Find each student's target heart range for exercise. Know the formula ... ?
220 - your age = _____ x .85 = _____(maximum heartrate)
Now take this # (the one above) x .75 =_____ (minimum heartrate)
During a workout, periodically take your pulse for 10 seconds, and then multiply it by 6. The number you get should be between the minimum and maximum heartrates.

57. As you listen to your heart and those of the folks around you, do you hear more than 1 sound? Listen for the "lub-dub." Research the valves on each side of the heart.

Closet Vibrato

The Experiment

This activity will transform a simple kite string and metal hanger into a deeply penetrating gong that will vibrate your inner soul. (Well, that is pushing it a bit, but after you are finished, you will be able to understand how vibrations can be transferred from one object or medium to another.)

Materials

1   Metal clothes hanger
1   Roll of kite string
1   Pair of scissors
1   Paper cup
1   Straight pin
1   Paper clip

PAPER CLIP

STRING

WAX CUP

Procedure

1. Push the straight pin through the middle of the bottom of the paper cup and make a small hole for the kite string to fit through.

2. Cut a piece of kite string to about 2 $^1/_2$ feet long. Poke one end through the hole and into the cup, and tie it to a paper clip inside the cup. Once you have the knot in the paper clip, tug it up inside the cup so it will not pull the string back through the cup. Use the illustration at the right as a guide.

3. Hold the hanger by the hook and pull down on the bottom of the hanger to change its shape from a triangle to a square or diamond. Tie the other end of the string to the hook of the hanger.

4. Let the hanger dangle freely as you hold the cup to your ear. Gently tap the hanger with the scissors and *voila'* ... INSTANT GONG! Once you listen to the sound that is produced for just a bit, you'll know where we came up with the name, "closet vibrato."

How Come, Huh?

Sound travels through solids, liquids, and gases by passing vibrations from one molecule to the next. Because the molecules are closer together in solids, the vibrations are passed from one molecule to another more efficiently. This transfers the sound without causing the energy to be lost from the source. As the scissors struck the hanger to begin the vibration, the energy traveled up the string and into the cup, where the vibration went from the solid string, to the paper clip, and then into the air within the cup. The vibrations in the cup were amplified and transferred to the air, where they were funneled into your ear and onto your eardrum. Next stop ... the brain.

Science Fair Extension

58. Try varying the size of the cups, string, and the materials that the cups are made from. Would styrofoam cups work better than paper? What about metal cups?

Aquarium Symphony

The Experiment

If you are doing the activities in the order in which they are presented in the book, you will see that we have beaten the sound-travels-through-solids idea nearly to death. With this lab, we are going to shift gears and explore the transmission of sound through liquids (specifically, water).

Materials

  1 Aquarium
10 Gallons of water
  1 Drinking glass, 12-16 oz.
  1 Metal fork
  1 Partner

Procedure

1. Fill the aquarium with 10 gallons of water.

2. Place your ear against the end of the aquarium, facing away from your lab partner, and listen as your partner taps the glass on the other end of the aquarium a number of times. Your job is to count how many times you hear a tap and tell your partner what you count. Use the illustration below as a guide.

3. Next, have your lab partner cup her hands and talk into the end of the aquarium. Listen and try to figure out what it is that your partner is saying. Use the illustration above as a guide.

4. Repeat the previous step, but this time, place a drinking glass on the end of the aquarium and ask your lab partner to talk to you through the other end again. Does the glass help or hinder the listening process?

How Come, Huh?

Water has a greater density than air, so it transmits sound more quickly. As the sound waves struck the glass, it started to vibrate, and caused the water molecules to vibrate, traveling across the water to the other pane of glass. When you placed the drinking glass on the pane, you were enlarging your collecting area. This should have enabled you to hear better.

Science Fair Extension

59. Grab your snorkel and mask. Jump into a swimming pool with a friend and experiment with sending sounds.

Sound Sponge

The Experiment

A sponge is an animal, or, in the case of modern production, a synthetic material, that absorbs liquids. A sound sponge, it stands to reason, is a material that soaks up sound. It absorbs sound so that it can not escape or be shared. This is precisely the point of this lab activity.

Sound can travel through solids, liquids, and gases but not through a vacuum. In a vacuum, there is nothing for the vibrating object to push on. There is no material to transfer the energy to. That is why space is a very quiet place ... unless you are watching the movies.

Materials

1   Vacuum pump
1   Bell jar with platform
1   Wind-up bell or buzzer

Procedure

1. Hook the vacuum pump up to the bell jar and make sure that it is properly evacuating air from inside.

2. Wind up a buzzer or bell and place it on the bell jar platform. Start the buzzer buzzing and place the bell jar over the buzzer. Because there is air inside the jar, you should be able to hear the buzzing sound produced by the vibrations.

3. Turn on the vacuum pump and start to remove air from inside the bell jar. Listen very carefully to the sound that is being made by the buzzer. You should notice that, as more and more air is removed from inside the jar, the sound is becoming quieter and quieter.

4. Continue to evacuate air until there is no more left inside the bell jar. At this point in time, the buzzer should still be vibrating away, but no audible sound should be transferred outside the bell jar.

5. Slowly release the stopcock on the vacuum pump, allowing air to seep back into the jar. As the amount of air increases, the volume of the bell should also increase.

How Come, Huh?

When there is no matter to push against or transfer energy to, then no sound can be passed along from one molecule to another. By removing all of the air from the inside of the bell jar, you removed the matter that the buzzer was going to push against. If there is no matter, then there is no way for sound waves to form.

Big Idea 7

Sound waves can be reflected.

Catch a Wave • Winholtz, Cramer, Twyman, & Hixson

Tuning Fork Echo

The Experiment
Matching the sound vibrations of a bottle with the vibrations of a tuning fork is not only fun, but it is also a great lesson in frequency and resonance. The challenge will be to get the same pitch from the bottle as from the tuning fork. This can be done with a little bit of patience, as well as some practice.

Materials
1   Glass milk bottle
1   Plastic tubing, 11" long
1   Tuning fork
1   Metric ruler
1   Buddy
     Water
     Good ears

Procedure
1. Fill the bottle with water, not quite to the top, and insert the piece of plastic tubing.

2. Strike the tuning fork and hold it above the top of the tube.

3. Move the tube up or down until the sound of the vibrating fork is amplified. When it sounds louder, you have produced the same pitch with the tube as with the tuning fork.

4. Hold it right there! Have your buddy measure the length of the tube that is above the water line.

Tuning Fork Echo

5. You can now calculate the wavelength. The wavelength of the tuning fork's note is 4 times the length of the part of the tube you measured. In other words:

(Length of tube above water x 4 = Wavelength of the tuning fork)

Data & Observations

According to your calculations, what is the wavelength of your tuning fork?

L = _____ cm x 4

L = _____

How Come, Huh?

When you hit the tuning fork, it vibrates at a specific frequency. This frequency produces sound waves that are an exact length each time.

When you hold the tuning fork above the plastic tube, those wavelengths enter the tube, hit the water inside the tube, and bounce back out the opening. In other words, they echo off the water. If the length of the tube is different from the length of the sound wave, the sound will still bounce off the water, but the waves will run into one another and will interfere with one another, thus making the sound quieter.

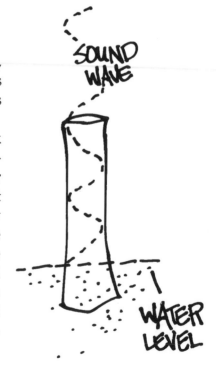

When you get the length of the tube just right, the waves actually slide by one another, and the sound is nice and clear. The tube is said to resonate, or vibrate, in unison with the sound waves. When this happens, the sound waves are going down, bouncing off the water, and returning up the tube along the same pathways. There is no banging into one another.

When you raise or lower the plastic tube, you are changing the length of the tube. The waves do not travel down, bounce, and return along unobstructed pathways.

Science Fair Extensions

60. Try bottles that have different-sized openings, and prove that the diameter of the bottle has no effect on the wavelength of the note that is produced by the tuning fork.

61. Try different liquids in your bottle—Karo syrup, ice water, hot water, alcohol—and see if the reflective surface has any effect on the sound waves that are reflected.

Bouncing Waves

The Experiment

The shortest distance between two points may be a straight line, but this activity will show you that taking the long way by bouncing off walls is more fun and educational. Using cardboard tubes and sound waves, you will play a kind of billiard game with sound.

Materials

2   Paper towel cardboard tubes, 12″ long
3   Pieces of poster board, approx. 5″ by 5″
1   Roll of tape
1   Egg carton
1   Pair of scissors
1   Wind-up kitchen timer
1   Protractor

Procedure

1. Using the scissors, cut apart the individual egg holders from the egg carton.

2. Place each cardboard tube on top of two egg holders, which will serve as bases, one on each end. Use tape to attach the tubes to these stands. Use the illustration below as a guide.

We have a fancy name for the tubes used in this lab. They are called TTBSs, or Tubes That Bounce Sound.

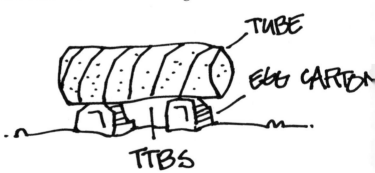

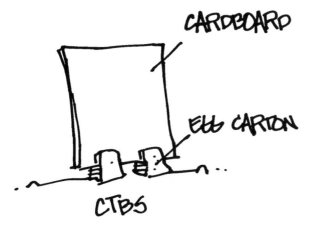

CARDBOARD

EGG CARTON

CTBS

3. Now, we are going to make CTBSs, or Cardboard That Bounces Sound. To make these high-tech scientific tools, you will make a cut right down the middle of the egg carton. Use the illustration at the left as a guide.

Once the cuts have been made, insert the piece of cardboard in one of the egg holders on one side. Place a second one on the other side. The illustration at the left will surely help.

4. Using the illustration below as a guide, place one of the CTBSs on the table with a TTBS pointing at it from a 45-degree angle. Place the other TTBS so that it points away at a 45-degree angle. Use the protractor to help you make accurate placements.

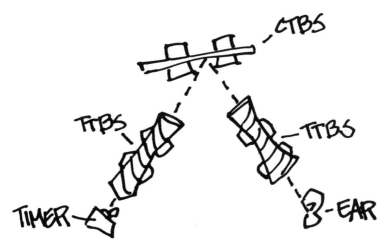

CTBS

TTBS

TTBS

TIMER

EAR

Bouncing Waves

5. Wind up the kitchen timer and place it at the opening of one TTBS. Place you ear at the other end of the TTBS and listen for the ticking that is produced by the timer.

6. Use the numbers in the Data & Observation section below and determine what the *Angle Out* is for each of the *Angle In* measurements.

7. Once you have taken all of the readings, use the other two CTBSs to bounce sound off two and three surfaces. You will need to line up the angles so that the sound actually can be bounced and collected. You should have enough experience to do that if you fill in the data table first.

Data & Observations

Angle In (A)	Angle Out (B)
45°	
30°	
70°	
10°	

How Come, Huh?

While sound waves can travel through solids, liquids, and gases, there is also a lot of bouncing going on. In this activity, the sound traveling away from the kitchen timer is vibrating out in all directions from it. Spreading out more and more as it gets farther from the timer, the tick-tock sound soon loses energy and cannot be heard very far from the source. When the timer is placed at one end of the tubing and your ear is positioned at the other end, the sound energy is collected by the tube and is concentrated. This concentrated sound energy cannot escape from the tunnels of the tubes. Therefore there is more energy in one direction, and it is focused. because there is little energy lost, the sound travels farther, bouncing off each CTBS and into the next tube until it reaches your ears, where the sound is collected, cataloged, and registered by the brain.

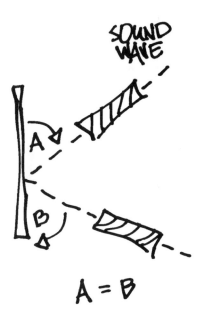

You also must think about both the surfaces of the CTBSs and the TTBSs. Because these surfaces are smooth and flat, the sound waves are reflected, or bounced, without losing much of the sound energy.

Science Fair Extensions

62. Try this with a rough-surfaced SCBS. What happens? Explain why the sound was not as clear as with the other surfaces.

63. See how many bounces off the CTBSs you can put in the path before you lose the sound.

Big Idea 8

Sound waves can be collected and amplified.

Catch a Wave • Winholtz, Cramer, Twyman, & Hixson

Animal Ears

The Experiment

How do animals know where we are before they see us ... ? Our smell, maybe ... but they can hear us before they see us. With this activity, you'll increase your hear-ability while raising some eyebrows with this tympanic membrane simulation. By attaching styrofoam cups to your ears, you increase the number of sound waves that your ears will capture. You will hear more like a 5th-grader waiting for school dismissal than your old Uncle Eddie.

Materials

6 Styrofoam cups
1 Pair of scissors

Procedure

1. Holding a cup carefully with one hand, make a cut that is approximately 3cm or one inch from the rim to the bottom.

2. At the end of the cut, draw a circle that is approximately the size of your ear. Cut out that circle.

3. Carefully place the cup onto your ear, so that the opening points in the same direction as your nose. Now you have increased the size of your outer ear, and you will be able to collect more good vibes. Check it out.

4. Compare listening to converstaions in the lunchroom with and without your ears. Go outside and do the same thing.

FRONT VIEW

CUP

SIDE VIEW

CUP

Animal Ears

How Come, Huh?

Your hearing is based on physical movements. First, sound waves must be directed into the ear. Then, these vibrations are funneled to the tympanic membrane (a.k.a. the "eardrum"). Ultimately the pressure changes against the eardrum turn into electrical signals that your brain interprets as sound.

This activity focuses on the pinna, or the outer part of the ear. This sound-collector appears in many shapes and sizes. From Dumbo to cauliflower ears, this structure catches waves by increasing the size of the pinna. By increasing the size of your pinna, you increase the number of vibrations you collect. The result is that you hear more, and everything you hear sounds louder.

As sound arrives at the ear, the pinna helps in determining where the sound is coming from—above, below, behind, or in front of you. If coming from the right, the right ear senses sound slightly before the left ear, and it sounds somewhat louder. This gives the owner of the ear a sense of the direction from which the sound has originated.

Try watching a variety of animals as they listen. Many animals, like dogs, have ears that can move independently of each other toward a sound. Like rotating satellite dishes, they can focus in on one direction or opposite directions to pinpoint the source of the sound.

Science Fair Extensions

64. Try this activity with different-sized pinna extenders (cups). Make these out of different materials.

65. Look into spy equipment. As a young boy, I purchased an electronic device called the "Big Ear." It was basically a microphone at the center of a satellite-dish-shaped thing. I could listen to my friends down the block. Figure out how this would work.

Portable Space Cannon

The Experiment

Is that an alien voice I hear? I don't think so. It's probably your lab partner creating some weird vibrations on a space cannon. This activity demonstrates sound but also emphasizes that you need matter in order to have sound. Do you think we could chat in outer space?

Materials

1   Metal Slinky
1   Pencil
1   Empty, plastic, 1-gallon milk jug
1   Pair of scissors
1   Pair of clean ears
1   Roll of masking tape
1   Partner

Procedure

1. Using the scissors, cut off the top third of the plastic milk jug. Be sure to recycle it.

2. Using the point of the scissors, punch a very small opening in the bottom of the jug.

3. Thread one end of the Slinky through the hole in the bottom of the jug. Tape it inside.

4. Give the other end of the Slinky to your partner. Ask your partner to gently stretch the spring out and away from you and the gallon jug that you are holding. Use the illustration at the right as a guide.

Portable Space Cannon

5. Hold the open end of the milk jug up near your ear and ask your partner to whap the spring with a pencil. Stretch the spring out and listen to the sound that is produced. Walk toward each other and let the spring droop a bit. Listen to the sound.

6. After you have used the pencil, ask your partner to flick the spring with a fingernail. Listen and record the quality of this new sound. Then have your partner whap the spring with the fleshy part of a finger. Record all your observations in the space below.

Data & Observations

Object	Sound Produced
Pencil	
Fingernail	
Finger	

How Come, Huh?

If we were in space, we wouldn't be able to hear one another. Why? No matter! In order for sound to travel, we have to have vibrations. If we are going to have vibrations, then we have to have something that will vibrate. That's where matter comes in. Different kinds of matter produce different kinds of

sound waves. Metal objects transmit sound very, very quickly, through a matrix of metal atoms that are highly ordered and have a great deal of structure. When the sound wave that was produced by the pencil whapping the spring reaches the plastic milk jug, it is collected and amplified. The metallic nature of the sound becomes greater. What you hear sounds like the cannons that we hear in the space movies.

Science Fair Extensions

66. You can change lots of variables in this experiment. Try different sizes of a) Slinky toys, b) milk jugs, c) milk jug materials, d) items to whap the spring.

67. Make a space phone using the Slinky instead of the string or the fishing line. If you have not made the soup can telephone yet, back up and try that lab. Then, adapt it to fit this idea.

Megaphone

The Experiment

Rah, rah, sis-boom-bah! That's right ... Stand and cheer for sound, but do it with a megaphone so you'll be heard. On second thought, you might want to do it in the privacy of your own home and possibly when you are alone. (Let's hope you have some dignity ... even though the authors don't.)

In this activity, you'll create a megaphone to demonstrate how sound waves can be focused to make a sound louder.

Materials

1   Sheet of butcher paper
1   Roll of masking tape
1   Pair of scissors

Procedure

1. Make a cone with your paper. Tape down the loose end of paper, as shown at the right.

2. With your scissors, cut off the mouthpiece (smaller end) so that it is about the same size as your mouth.

3. Trim the larger end with your scissors so that it looks round and can stand on its own. When you are all done making your megaphone, hold it up and holler into it.

How Come, Huh?

Have you noticed that before you yell at a football game, to your friends, or at some beanhead who irritates you, you often place your hands on either side of your mouth? You are creating your own megaphone. A megaphone makes sound louder by concentrating or focusing the sound energy in one direction. Without being guided through the funnel-shaped border of the megaphone, our sound vibrations leave our mouths in almost all directions. That energy is spread thin. However when sound energy is focused, it travels farther and sounds louder.

Science Fair Extension

68. Prove that the diameter of the opening of the megaphone is directly proportional to the volume of the sound produced.

Gramophone Cone

The Experiment

At first blush, you probably think you are going to build an instrument that will help you to summon little old ladies. This is not the case.

The gramophone was invented in the late 1800s by Thomas Edison. Sound recordings were made on wax cylinders and then placed on a spindle, or spool. A needle was placed on the wax recording, and as the spool rotated slowly, the marking in the wax caused the needle to vibrate up and down. These vibrations were then collected by a large cone and amplified.

You are going to make a crude replica of this instrument by attaching a sewing needle to the end of a large paper cone and "playing" an old record with it.

Materials

1   Sewing needle
1   Roll of transparent tape
1   Sheet of butcher paper
1   Old record player
1   Old record

CONE

NEEDLE

Procedure

1. Make a cone, using the same pattern that you used when you made the megaphone (previous lab). This cone should be only about half the size of the megaphone.

2. Tape the needle to the bottom of the cone, referring to the illustration at the left.

3. With your parents' permission, find an old used phonograph record and place it on the turn-table of a record player.

4. Start the record spinning and gently place the needle in the grooves on the outside edge of the record. Support the cone and needle but do not try to put any pressure on the needle while it is on the record.

The needle will quickly settle into one of the grooves that you see in the record's surface. Listen to the sound that is collected and amplified through your paper cone.

How Come, Huh?

The surface of the record is full of tiny bumps. When the needle is placed in a groove, it bounces and jumps as it moves over these bumps. This causes the needle to vibrate. Think of a car bouncing down a dusty old country road, and you'll get the idea. The needle starts to vibrate and sends those vibrations to the paper. The paper picks those vibrations up and amplifies them so that we can hear them.

Science Fair Extension

69. Listen to the record at different speeds. With luck, your player will work at 33, 45, and 78 rpms (revolutions per minute). What happens as you speed up the record?

Chicken in a Cup

The Experiment

Sound is produced when an object vibrates. To take advantage of this idea and also tie it into a fun art project, we are going to make a chicken in a cup. This, in no way, is related to the chicken on a stick found in the taste lab section of another book.

Materials

1   5-oz. wax cup
1   12" length of string
1   Paper clip
1   Pair of fingers
1   Piece of masking tape
    Water

Procedure

1. Open the paper clip up and punch a small hole in the center of the bottom of the wax cup. Put the end of the string over the hole and push it through to the other side, using the paper clip. The idea is to keep the hole as small as possible so that more of the vibration is transferred to the cup and is amplified.

2. Tie the paper clip to the outside end of the string. Reach into the cup and pull the string snug so that the paper clip is right on the bottom of the cup. Tape the paper clip to the bottom of the cup.

3.   Grab the string with your thumb and forefinger near the bottom of the cup. Pull downward with short pulls and listen. Little to no sound should be produced.

4.   Now, wet the string with the water, and pull it down again. With a little bit of practice, you will be winning the chicken-calling contest at the state fair.

How Come, Huh?

PULL
DOWN

The water on your fingers creates friction between your skin and the cotton string. The friction produces tiny vibrations, which travel up the string. When they hit the bottom of the cup, the cup starts to vibrate and this is amplified by the shape of the cup. Good luck at the county fair!

Science Fair Extensions

70. Adapt the components of the experiment to produce different kinds of sounds. Change the size and material that the cup is made from, and change the material you pull on. You might try string, fishing line, twine, or even a thin piece of wire. Compare the sounds that are produced.

71. Make chickens of different pitches, decorate your cups, and have a chicken symphony with your friends.

Thunder Drums

The Experiment

Thunder drum is the commercial name given to a sound effects device used in theaters. It is a large cardboard cylinder, cut at a 45° angle at one end. It is also covered with the same material that drum-makers use to produce snare drums.

In the middle of the drum head is a long, thin spring that is attached in the middle and hangs freely outside the cylinder. The illustration at the left should give you a good idea of what we are talking about. The person creating the "thunder" slides a hand in the hand grip and shakes the drum back and forth. As the spring vibrates, it passes those vibrations to the drum head, which, in turn, passes them to the air. The resulting sound is somewhat like the thunder that follows a bolt of lightning.

We are going to make a homemade version of the same thing.

Materials

1 Small thunder drum
1 Large thunder drum
1 Ice cream container, 1 gallon
1 Pair of scissors
1 Sheet of hard plastic
1 Spring, 18", slender
1 Piece of masking tape

Procedure

1. Using the illustration at the right as a guide, cut a 30° angle in the end of the ice cream container.

2. Place the cut end of the carton down on a piece of hard plastic. Trace around the outside of the carton.

3. Cut the plastic out and tape it over the cut end of the carton.

4. Make a small hole in the center of the plastic with the scissors, and wiggle the spring into the hole so that the main part of the spring is outside the carton. Tape the spring in place.

5. Pick up your homemade thunder drum with both hands and give it a shake. You'll find that it's almost as good as the real thing.

How Come, Huh?

The spring vibrates, the vibrations push on the plastic, and the plastic pushes on the air. It's thunder in a bucket ... for cheap!

Science Fair Extension

72. Make thunder drums of different sizes and out of different materials. Explore, question, prod, poke, and have fun with this idea.

CUT HERE

CARDBOARD GALLON

PLASTIC

SPRING

Big Idea 9

Sound waves can be absorbed. If the object absorbing the sound is resonant with the object that is producing the waves, that object may also produce the same sound.

Eggsorbing Sound

The Experiment

This is an eggcellent way to demonstrate sound-proofing and to see how sound waves travel. Listening to sounds through a smooth-sided box is different from listening to sounds through the same box lined with egg cartons. This is different still from the way sounds travel inside a box that has cotton balls on its sides.

You will construct your own examples and listen for yourself to see how sound is bounced, collected, and absorbed by different materials.

Materials

3   Shoeboxes (same size)
1   Pair of scissors
2   Styrofoam egg cartons
1   Bag of cotton balls
1   Bottle of glue, or 1 glue gun
1   Kitchen timer

Procedure

1. Remove the lids from all three of the shoeboxes. Cut 1 hole in each end of the box.

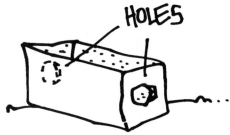

2. Line the second box with egg cartons. Cut and glue them around the inside of the box so that most of the wallspace inside the box is covered with styrofoam.

Eggsorbing Sound

3. Line the inside of the third box with cotton balls. Glue them around the inside of the box so that most of the wallspace inside the box is covered.

4. Place the first box (the one that is empty) on the table. Wind up the kitchen timer so that it starts ticking. Place the timer in front of one hole on the opposite side of the box. Use the illustration above as a guide. Listen to the volume of the sound transmitted through the box. Rate the sound from 1, being barely audible, to 5, being very loud and easy to hear.

5. Record the volume of the timer as you listen to the sound of the timer through all three boxes.

Data & Observations

Sound-Proofing	Volume
Empty box	
Egg carton	
Cotton balls	

How Come, Huh?

Sound travels in waves. The waves move kind of like the last kid in the lunch line, pushing the kid in front of him. That kid pushes the next kid, and so it continues, until the kid at the front of the line slams into *your* back. Yep, that's a sound wave!

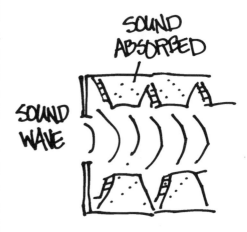

Sounds are produced by vibrations. Sound travels best through solid things, because they transmit vibrations easily. When sound waves are being transmitted through the air, they can bounce into other things that get in the way— like the egg-carton mountains. The sound waves strike the sides of the carton and get absorbed; therefore, the sound is muffled.

This is kind of like shouting in an empty room, singing in the shower, or yelling down a deep, steep cavern. Sound waves bounce off the flat, straight surfaces and back to the listener's ears. There is nothing to trap or absorb the waves as they bounce from surface to surface.

Science Fair Extension

73. Create other sound-absorbing boxes using different materials: How about popcorn, styrofoam, plastic bags, cups, and paper wads? Let your imagination run wild. That is how new products evolve and make it to the marketplace.

Resonant Rods

The Experiment

This experiment provides the opportunity for you to learn about harmonic, or resonant, sound vibrations by actually seeing them.

It comes from a book published by the good folks at the Exploratorium in San Francisco. The book is called *The Spinning Blackboard* and it is full of science snacks that have been tested by teachers and kids. (You know that the experiments will work.)

In this lab, four wooden dowels of varying lengths are each topped with an identical weight. These four dowels are then rocked back and forth together, and when the vibration caused by you matches the resonant frequency of one of the dowels, that dowel vibrates back forth in a wide arc. It resonates.

Materials

3   1/4 inch wooden dowels,
      1-1/2 feet (45cm) long,
      2 feet (60cm) long, and
      2-1/2 feet (75cm) long
1   3/4 inch (9.5mm) dowel
      2 feet (60cm) long
4   Superballs, large
1   2 by 4 board
      approximately 2 feet long
1   Electric drill
1   Vice

Procedure

1. Drill four holes, approximately 4 inches apart, down the center of the 2 x 4 (board).

The first three holes should be smaller than 1/4 inch, and the fourth hole should be just a bit smaller than 3/8 inch.

2. Gently wiggle, shovel and cajole the dowels into the holes so that they are held firmly in place.

3. Using the drill, carefully make a 1/4 inch hole halfway through three of the Superballs, and a 3/8 inch (9.5mm) hole halfway through the fourth. Use a vice to keep the balls from moving around.

4. Place one Superball on the end of each dowel.

5. Grab the board at each end and slide it back and forth sideways across the tabletop. As you vary the rate at which you move the board, different dowels will swing back and forth at different rates. Some will move with great amplitude; others may hardly move at all.

6. Move the board at different speeds and compare how each of the dowels move. Write a general rule that correlates length with the resonant frequency of the dowel.

Resonant Rods

How Come, Huh?

When you find the resonant frequency of any object, the amplitude of the vibration, the size of it, and how much it moves back and forth all become very large.

Some common examples of this can be found on the playground. When you push someone in a swing and you match your push to the back-and-forth motion of the swing, the amplitude of the swing gets larger and larger. The same thing happens when you get a good string of attacks going on the tetherball court: You hit the ball and it goes faster and faster and higher and higher, and you use your knowledge of physics to whip your opponent.

Resonance has been responsible for the destruction of buildings during earthquakes and bridges during windstorms. When an army marches across a bridge, soldiers break cadence and walk in irregular strides so that the resonant period of the bridge does not start moving the bridge up and down.

Science Fair Extension

74. Repeat the experiment without the balls and see if takes more energy or less to find the resonant frequencies.

Resonant Cylinders

The Experiment

You may need some extra hands on deck for this slippery demo. A tuning fork is struck and held over a graduated cylinder that has a tube of PVC pipe inside it. The height of the PVC pipe is moved up and down until the tuning fork vibration resonates with the air column inside the pipe. This amplifies the sound vibrations that are produced by the fork.

Materials

1   1,000ml graduated cylinder
1   PVC pipe, $^1/_2$" diam, 12" long
3   Tuning forks, different frequencies
1   Partner
1   Metric ruler
     Water

Procedure

1. Put 700ml of water in the graduated cylinder.

2. Ask your partner to slide the PVC pipe inside the cylinder.

3. Whap the tuning fork on your thigh and hold it over the PVC pipe with the fingers, or tines, of the fork pointing down into the cylinder. **Do not touch the PVC pipe with the tuning fork.**

4. Slowly move the PVC pipe up and down until the sound that is produced by the fork is amplified.

Resonant Cylinders

5. Experiment with different forks and find and measure the distance that is required for the fork to resonate.

Data & Observations

Tuning Fork	Resonant Depth
1.	
2.	
3.	

How Come, Huh?

The vibrating tuning fork causes the air column inside the PVC pipe to vibrate. As the PVC pipe is lifted, the length of the air column is changed. When the air column length resonates with the vibrations of the tuning fork, the amplitude of the vibrations produces a loud note. If you continue to lift the PVC pipe, you will pass the resonant point.

Science Fair Extensions

75. Use the tuning fork to make other objects vibrate. Will other tuning forks pick up the vibration? What about a guitar string or a piano string?

76. Graph the tuning fork frequency compared to the length of the resonant air column.

Resonant Bottles

The Experiment

This is a great demo, so be patient and strive for success. This is a great example of a good vibration. By "tuning" a bottle filled with water, you can duplicate the note made by a tuning fork.

In addition to being able to match the pitch of a tuning fork, you can also fill two bottles to the same level. When you get the air to vibrate and produce a sound in one, it will duplicate that sound in the second bottle, which matches and sits near the first.

Materials

4 Glass bottles, 12 oz.
1 Tuning fork
2 Good ears
1 Partner
Water

Procedure

1. First you need to tune your bottle. Strike the tuning fork and then blow across the top of the bottle. Do you produce the same "note"? Adding water to the bottle will raise the pitch. Add some water and continue to blow and strike the tuning fork until the notes match.

Resonant Bottles

2. When the bottle's note is at the same pitch as the fork, the air in the bottle should begin to vibrate back and forth. If you are doing the activities in this book in order, you should have a pretty good idea of what resonance is and why your bottle is humming.

3. Once you get the resonant note set up, fill a second bottle with the same amount of water as the first.

4. Pucker up and blow across the bottle that you just filled. Have your partner listen to the other bottle. (We are thinking that the illustration at the bottom of the page pretty much sums up this step.) Ask your partner to listen for the same note that you produced. If the bottle is tuned properly, it will resonate and produce the same note.

How Come, Huh?

When you whapped the tuning fork and got it to resonate with the bottle, the sound waves produced by the fork were the same length as the space in the bottle, so they resonated.

When you blew across the resonant bottle and the person listening to the other bottle heard the same note, it was for the same reason. The sound produced by the first bottle was the same length as the space in the second bottle, so it resonated. This works on holidays and after hours, too!

Science Fair Extensions

77. Considering resonance is important when making musical instruments, as well as when designing music halls. Find knowledgeable people to share information with you. For example, talk with band/orchestra leaders, workers in music stores, and workers in concert halls. Figure out what makes for a good performance hall and what does not.

The Tabernacle in Salt Lake City, UT, is so well designed acoustically that a person can stand at the very front of the building, by the conductor's podium, brush the sleeve of a suit coat, and the folks at the very back of the room can hear it clearly.

Big Idea 10

Variations in wave patterns can produce phenomena like bangs, explosions, sonic booms, and the Doppler Effect.

Paper Poppers

The Experiment

Generations have made and used the paper popper as an entertaining party game without recognizing its educational value. With this activity, you will construct a paper popper, use it to demonstrate the action and sound it creates, and annoy all of the parakeets in the general vicinity.

Materials

1   Square of paper
1   Pair of scissors

Procedure

1. Fold the top, left-hand corner of the paper over to form a triangle. There will be illustrations for each of the steps, so take a peek, pay attention, and this will be a breeze.

2. Tear or cut the bottom off the paper that you folded.

3. Rotate the triangle so that it looks like the second illustration at the right. Grab the top sheet only and fold the top right-hand corner down about an inch.

4. Fold the triangle in half again. Make sure that the corner that you already folded in is inside the fold that you make this time.

Paper Poppers

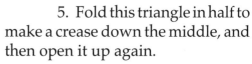

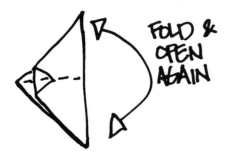

5. Fold this triangle in half to make a crease down the middle, and then open it up again.

6. Now, fold the top half of the triangle up, and crease it.

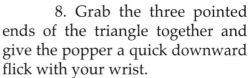

7. Flip the whole popper over. Fold the other side up. Crease it.

8. Grab the three pointed ends of the triangle together and give the popper a quick downward flick with your wrist.

Hang on to the popper. It does not make a sound by throwing it. It requires the quick snap of a wrist, instead. The paper folded under should be caught by the air and pushed out quickly. When this happens, the paper will snap and produce a "pop."

If is does not work the first time, keep trying. Practice will pay off with success.

How Come, Huh?

When you bring the popper down quickly, the air catches the piece of paper inside and pulls it out quickly. The paper pushes on the air and produces a vibration.

The volume of the vibration and the loudness of the pop are dependent on how quick you are with your wrist and how fast the paper opens up. The quicker you are and the faster the paper strikes the air, the louder the pop will be.

A whip works in much the same way. When a ranch hand or *vaquero* takes a whip and snaps it, you will hear a loud pop. This is the sound of the end of the whip snapping back on itself at very high speeds, sometimes in excess of 500 miles per hour. When the leather snaps against the air, the air is struck with a very fast moving wave, which travels out from the whip and is percieved by our ears as a "pop."

Science Fair Extension

78. Use different materials and try different-sized poppers. What happens to the sound of the popper as the size increases? Does the material really make a difference? (Is a satin hanky any different from a leather bootstrap?) Curious minds want to know.

Baster Blaster

The Experiment

You can demonstrate how thunder is created and make Thanksgiving a whole lot more fun in your house at the same time. This experiment allows you to create a controlled reaction in a rubber bulb that will launch a Ping-Pong ball into the air with a loud bang. The lab demonstrates how superheated air expands rapidly, causing a bang. Thunder is produced in the same way.

Materials

1   Turkey baster
1   Kitchen knife
1   Lantern ignitor
1   Ping-Pong ball
1   Eyedropper
1   Bottle of isopropyl alcohol
    Adult supervision

Procedure

1. Remove the rubber bulb from a turkey baster. Using a sharp kitchen knife, carefully cut a small "X" in the side of the bulb. Use the illustration at the right to help you locate the correct spot.

2. A lantern ignitor can be purchased from a sporting goods store. Remove the nut from the end and thread the shaft through the "X" that you made in the side of the bulb. Replace the nut. Use the illustration to the right as a guide.

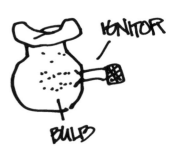

3. Squeeze the center of an eyedropper that is full of isopropyl alcohol inside the bulb and swirl it around a bit.

4. Place the Ping-Pong ball inside the opening of the baster.

5. Pointing the ball away from yourself and others, give the ignitor a quick twist and the ball will shoot into the air with a loud, high pop.

How Come, Huh?

Isopropyl alcohol is a flammable liquid. When you squirted the liquid into the rubber bulb, it started to vaporize almost instantly, making it even more flammable.

Placing the Ping-Pong ball in the mouth of the baster created a closed system, trapping the flammable gas inside the bulb. When you flipped the ignitor switch, a spark was generated. The spark ignited the alcohol vapor 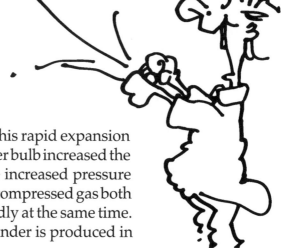 which expanded rapidly. This rapid expansion of heated gas inside the baster bulb increased the pressure dramatically. The increased pressure pushed the ball out and the compressed gas both escaped and expanded rapidly at the same time. This produced a bang. Thunder is produced in a similar way.

Science Fair Extension

79. Take the idea and adapt it to different-sized containers with different balls. Nerf balls work great because you can cram them into small spaces. Use your imagination and work carefully.

Sonic Airburst Booms

The Experiment

The Air Burst rocket is a relatively new product to come out on the market, introduced at Toy Fair in 2001. It is a water-and-air-powered rocket that shoots over 1000 feet into the air. This is cool, but the really cool thing is, that, when the rocket is launched, there is a loud "bang." When the folks at Cal Tech studied the rocket, they determined that the reason for the bang was that the water leaving the bottom of the rocket was moving faster than the speed of sound. This was causing a mini sonic boom.

Materials

1   Air Burst rocket
1   Bicycle pump
1   Large, open field
    Water

Procedure

1. Using the directions that are provided in the box, assemble the rocket launcher and rocket.

2. Start with a single membrane so that you get the feel for the rocket and so that you don't loose it when you shoot it the first time.

3. Launch the rocket and listen for the sonic boom that is produced when the rocket shoots off into the air.

4. Experiment to see if the size of the sonic boom is in any way correlated to the number of membranes you use.

How Come, Huh?

When an object is producing sound, the waves move out and away from that object. As the air and water start to rush out of the bottom of the rocket, they produce sound waves. The water and air are moving so fast that they not only catch, but pass, the sound waves that they produce. This compresses, or squeezes, the sound waves together, and this is what causes the "boom."

The speed of sound was once dubbed the "sound barrier," and it was thought to be like a wall. No one could go faster than the speed of sound. If they tried, they would run into this "wall" and get mooshed. In 1947, a test pilot named Chuck Yeager, flying a rocket plane designed by Bell Labs, flew faster than the speed of sound. When the plane broke the sound barrier, it produced the first sonic boom. Observers on the ground thought that Capt. Yeager had died. A couple of seconds later, he radioed down that, not only was he alive and well, but that the boom had broken his Mach Meter, the instrument that measures how fast the plane is flying.

Science Fair Extension

80. Create a model that shows what happens to sound waves during a sonic boom.

Doppler Demo

The Experiment

All kids know the sound of a car passing in front of them on a race track … even if they've never been to the Indy-500. I would bet that 99% of your friends can make that sound, if you ask them. This is a racy way to learn about the Doppler Effect. You will use embroidery hoops or create your own paper loop sound waves to demonstrate how the idea works.

Pretend you have front-row seats at the Indy-500. Can you imitate the sound the cars make as they speed by in front of you? The pitch seems to go from high to low, but do you know why? When sound waves are bunched up in the front of a car, they create a high-frequency pitch. When they are spread out in the back of the car, they create a lower-frequency pitch. Using circles of various sizes, you can demonstrate this Doppler Effect.

Materials

5 Construction paper strips, 1" thick, 11" long
1 Pair of scissors
1 Small toy car
1 Bottle of glue

Procedure

1. The paper should be cut from a standard sheet of construction paper. We will to assume that the longest piece is 11" long. Cut strips of 10", 9", 8", and 7".

2. Connect the ends of the paper strips, making loops out of each one. Then place the rings, one inside the other. Use the illustration shown here as a guide.

3. Place the small car in the center of the rings, and "drive" it to one side of the rings.

4. The rings should bunch up in front of the car and spread out in the back of the car. You have just created a visual model of what happens to sound waves as a car passes in front of you very quickly.

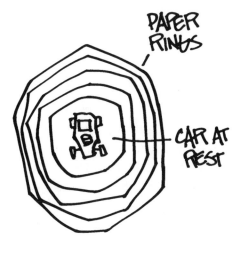

PAPER RINGS

CAR AT REST

How Come, Huh?

When a car is idling, sitting still with the engine running, the sound waves travel out in all directions equally, relative to the position of the car. That would be the first arrangement of rings (sound waves) and your car.

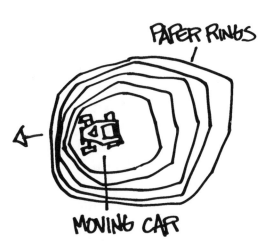

PAPER RINGS

MOVING CAR

Doppler Demo

As the car travels forward, it moves away from one edge of the first sound wave and toward the other. At the same time that the car is moving, it is also producing another sound wave. This second sound wave is not spaced equally, like when the car was idling. Instead, it is a little closer to one side and a little farther from the other.

The car moves again. It gets closer still to one side of the first sound, and farther from the other. When sound waves bunch up and get closer together, they produce a higher pitch. So, when a car traveling really fast comes toward you, the sound waves are bunched up, and they produce a high pitch.

SOUND WAVES BUNCHED (HIGH)

SOUND WAVES SPREAD OUT (LOW)

After the car passes you, the waves are spreading out. The farther apart the waves are, the lower the pitch that is produced. That's where you get the Doppler Effect. The sound starts high because the waves are all scrunched together. When the vehicle passes, the waves spread out, and the pitch gets lower rapidly.

Science Fair Extension

81. Head outside and collect actual recordings of the Doppler Effect. Be sure to use caution if you are near a roadway where cars and trucks are traveling at high speeds. You may also want to go the airport, where planes are taking off and landing. This is another excellent place to hear the Doppler Effect first-hand.

Instead of engine noises, collect siren sounds from police cars, ambulances, or fire stations.

Doppler's Mosquito

The Experiment

The final lab in this book is a demonstration of the Doppler Effect. All kids love to whirl things over their heads and make noise. If that's your bag, this lab is for you.

An artificial insect, which we are calling Doppler's Mosquito, is made using a paint stick, rubber band, and a cork. The best part about this creation is that it actually buzzes like a giant mosquito.

Materials

1   Paint stick
1   Cork
1   Knife
1   Rubber band, large, fat
1   Pair of scissors
1   Hot glue gun
1   Gluestick
1   Box of colored markers
1   Spool of string
1   Pair of goggles

Procedure

1.   Cut a medium-sized cork in half and notch the inside just a bit.

2.   Place your paint stick in the notches, and add a bit of hot glue to hold the two halves in place.

3.   Carefully place the rubber band around the outside of the cork. (Get a partner to help you with this part so that you do not disturb your glue while it is drying.)

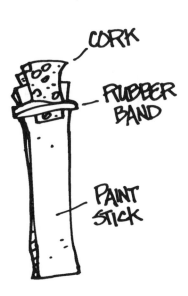

CORK

RUBBER BAND

PAINT STICK

Doppler's Mosquito

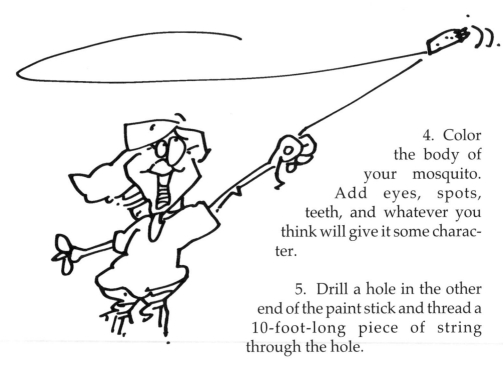

4. Color the body of your mosquito. Add eyes, spots, teeth, and whatever you think will give it some character.

5. Drill a hole in the other end of the paint stick and thread a 10-foot-long piece of string through the hole.

6. Double the string up and knot it so that you have a 5-foot-long piece of string hanging off the end of your mosquito.

7. Put on your goggles and get in an open space. Whirl the mosquito slowly around your head. Listen to the sound that you hear.

8. Now speed it up. Do you hear a different sound? Describe the two sounds, and explain how Doppler would describe the position and location of the sound waves as the mosquito whirled around your head.

9. Vary the length of the string and see if it has any effect on the sound waves and the pitch of the sound that is produced.

Science Fair Extension

82. Make a bull-roarer. You will need the following items:

1   Paper tube
1   Spool of string
1   Pair of scissors
1   Piece of elastic, 24" long

A. Thread the elastic through the paper tube and tie it off.

B. Cut a 10-foot piece of string. Double it up and tie it to the elastic.

C. Whirl the bull-roarer over your head at different speeds and with different lengths of string. Listen to the sound that is produced and compare that sound to the sound made by your mosquito.

That's it. Thanks for reading all the way through the book. We've been glad to share ideas with you, and we hope that you will try one of the other books in the series.

Science Fair Projects
•
A Step-by-Step Guide: From Idea To Presentation

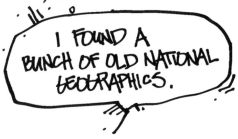

Science Fair Projects

Ah, the impending science fair project—a good science fair project has the following five characteristics:

1. The student must come up with an *original* question.
2. That *original* question must be suited to an experiment in order to provide an answer.
3. The *original* idea is outlined with just one variable isolated.
4. The *original* experiment is performed and documented using the scientific method.
5. A presentation of the *original* idea in the form of a lab write-up and display board is completed.

Science Fair Projects

As simple as science fair versus science project sounds, it gets screwed up millions of times a year by sweet, unsuspecting students who are counseled by sweet, unknowing, and probably just-as-confused parents.

To give you a sense of contrast, we have provided a list of legitimate science fair projects and then reports that do not qualify. We will also add some comments in italics that should help clarify why they do or do not qualify in the science fair project department.

Science Fair Projects

1. Temperature and the amount of time it takes mealworms to change to beetles.

Great start. We have chosen a single variable that is easy to measure: temperature. From this point forward the student can read, explore, and formulate an original question that is the foundation for the project.

A colleague of mine actually did a similar type of experiment for his master's degree. His topic: The rate of development of fly larvae in cow poop as a function of temperature. No kidding. He found out that the warmer the temperature of the poop, the faster the larvae developed into flies.

2. The effect of different concentrations of soapy water on seed germination.

Again, wonderful. Measuring the concentration of soapy water. This leads naturally into original questions and a good project.

3. Crystal size and the amount of sugar in the solution.

This could lead into other factors such as exploring the temperature of the solution, the size of the solution container, and other variables that may affect crystal growth. Opens a lot of doors.

vs. Science Reports

4. Helicopter rotor size and the speed at which it falls.

Size also means surface area, which is very easy to measure. The student who did this not only found the mathematical threshold with relationship to air friction, but she had a ton of fun.

5. The ideal ratio of baking soda to vinegar to make a fire extinguisher.

Another great start. Easy to measure and track, leads to a logical question that can either be supported or refuted with the data.

Each of those topics *measures* one thing, such as the amount of sugar, the concentration of soapy water, or the ideal size. If you start with an idea that allows you to measure something, then you can change it, ask questions, explore, and ultimately make a *prediction*, also called a *hypothesis*, and experiment to find out if you are correct. As a contrast, here are some well-meaning but misguided entries:

Science Reports, <u>not Projects</u>
1. Dinosaurs!

OK, great. Everyone loves dinosaurs but where is the experiment? Did you find a new dinosaur? Is Jurassic Park alive and well, and we are headed there to breed, drug, or in some way test them? Probably not. This was a report on T. rex. Cool, but not a science fair project. And judging by the protest that this kid's mom put up when the kid didn't get his usual"A", it is a safe bet that she put a lot of time in and shared in the disappointment.

More Reports &

2. Our Friend the Sun

Another very large topic, no pun intended. This could be a great topic. Sunlight is fascinating. It can be split, polarized, reflected, refracted, measured, collected, converted. However, this poor kid simply chose to write about the size of the sun, regurgitating facts about its features, cycles, and other astrofacts while simultaneously offending the American Melanoma Survivors Society. Just kidding about that last part.

3. Smokers' Poll

A lot of folks think that they are headed in the right direction here. Again, it depends on how the kid attacks the idea. Are they going to single out race? Heredity? Shoe size? What exactly are they after here? The young lady who did this report chose to make it more of a psychology-studies effort than a scientific report. She wanted to know family income, if they fought with their parents, how much stress was on the job, and so on. All legitimate concerns but not placed in the right slot.

4. The Majestic Moose

If you went out and caught the moose, drugged it to see the side effects for disease control, or even mated it with an elk to determine if you could create an animal that would become the spokesanimal for the Alabama Dairy Farmers' Got Melk? promotion, that would be fine. But, another fact-filled report should be filed with the English teacher.

5. How Tadpoles Change into Frogs

Great start, but they forgot to finish the statement. We know how tadpoles change into frogs. What we don't know is how tadpoles change into frogs if they are in an altered environment, if they are hatched out of cycle, if they are stuck under the tire of an off-road vehicle blatantly driving through a protected wetland area. That's what we want to know. How tadpoles change into frogs, if, when, or under what measurable circumstances.

Now that we have beaten the chicken squat out of this introduction, we are going to show you how to pick a topic that can be adapted to become a successful science fair project after one more thought.

One Final Comment

A Gentle Reminder

Quite often I discuss the scientific method with moms and dads, teachers and kids, and get the impression that, according to their understanding, there is one, and only one, scientific method. This is not necessarily true. There are lots of ways to investigate the world we live in and on.

Paleontologists dig up dead animals and plants but have no way to conduct experiments on them. They're dead. Albert Einstein, the most famous scientist of the last century and probably on everybody's starting five of all time, never did experiments. He was a theoretical physicist, which means that he came up with a hypothesis, skipped over collecting materials for things like black holes and space-time continuums, didn't experiment on anything or even collect data. He just went straight from hypothesis to conclusion, and he's still considered part of the scientific community. You'll probably follow the six steps we outline but keep an open mind.

Project Planner

This outline is designed to give you a specific set of timelines to follow as you develop your science fair project. Most teachers will give you 8 to 11 weeks' notice for this kind of assignment. We are going to operate from the shorter timeline with our suggested schedule, which means that the first thing you need to do is get a calendar.

A. The suggested time to be devoted to each item is listed in parentheses next to that item. Enter the date of the Science Fair and then, using the calendar, work backward, entering dates.

B. As you complete each item, enter the date that you completed it in the column between the goal (due date) and project item.

Goal   *Completed*   *Project Item*

1. Generate a Hypothesis (2 weeks)

Goal	Completed	Project Item
_____	_____	Review Idea Section, pp. 196–201
_____	_____	Try Several Experiments
_____	_____	Hypothesis Generated
_____	_____	Finished Hypothesis Submitted
_____	_____	Hypothesis Approved

2. Gather Background Information (1 week)

Goal	Completed	Project Item
_____	_____	Concepts / Discoveries Written Up
_____	_____	Vocabulary / Glossary Completed
_____	_____	Famous Scientists in Field

& Timeline

Goal Completed Project Item

3. Design an Experiment (1 week)

_____	_____	Procedure Written
_____	_____	Lab Safety Review Completed
_____	_____	Procedure Approved
_____	_____	Data Tables Prepared
_____	_____	Materials List Completed
_____	_____	Materials Acquired

4. Perform the Experiment (2 weeks)

_____	_____	Scheduled Lab Time

5. Collect and Record Experimental Data (part of 4)

_____	_____	Data Tables Completed
_____	_____	Graphs Completed
_____	_____	Other Data Collected and Prepared

6. Present Your Findings (2 weeks)

_____	_____	Rough Draft of Paper Completed
_____	_____	Proofreading Completed
_____	_____	Final Report Completed
_____	_____	Display Completed
_____	_____	Oral Report Outlined on Index Cards
_____	_____	Practice Presentation of Oral Report
_____	_____	Oral Report Presentation
_____	_____	Science Fair Setup
_____	_____	Show Time!

Scientific Method
• Step 1 •
The Hypothesis

Catch a Wave • Winholtz, Cramer, Twyman, & Hixson

The Hypothesis

A hypothesis is an educated guess. It is a statement of what you think will probably happen. It is also the most important part of your science fair project because it directs the entire process. It determines what you study, the materials you will need, and how the experiment will be designed, carried out, and evaluated. Needless to say, you need to put some thought into this part.

There are four steps to generating a hypothesis:

Step One • Pick a Topic
Preferably something that you are interested in studying. We would like to politely recommend that you take a peek at physical science ideas (physics and chemistry) if you are a rookie and this is one of your first shots at a science fair project. These kinds of lab ideas allow you to repeat experiments quickly. There is a lot of data that can be collected, and there is a huge variety to choose from.

If you are having trouble finding an idea, all you have to do is pick up a compilation of science activities (like this one) and start thumbing through it. Go to the local library or head to a bookstore and you will find a wide and ever-changing selection to choose from. Find a topic that interests you and start reading. At some point, an idea will catch your eye, and you will be off to the races.

Pick An Idea You Like

We hope you find an idea you like between the covers of this book. But we also realize that 1) there are more ideas about sound than we have included in this book, and 2) other kinds of presentations, or methods of writing labs, may be just what you need to trigger a new idea or put a different spin on things. So, without further ado …

For Older Kids …

1. Sound FUNdamentals. Funtastic Science Activities for Kids Written by Robert W. Wood. Illustrated by Rick Brown. ISBN 0-7910-4840-3. Published by Chelsea House Publishers. 124 pages.

A great book for older elementary and intermediate school age kids. The book contains 29 activities that are written in a clear and entertaining style. Humorous illustrations give valuable clues to the kids to help them to do the activities, which all have clever names, and each lab is followed by a section titled, "Guess What?" These are fun facts and science trivia that add to each lab.

2. Awesome Experiments in Light and Sound. Written by Michael DiSpezio. Illustrated by Catherine Leary. ISBN 0-8069-9823-7. Published by Sterling Publishing Company. 160 pages.

This is an excellent resource for both sound and light. Thirty-four lab activities are presented in a clear and concise manner. The author has also added fun facts to go with the clear illustrations, which are very well done. There are also great extension ideas.

3. Physics for Every Kid. Written by Janice Van Cleave. ISBN 0-471-52505-7. Published by John Wiley & Sons. 192 pages.

Sound is one topic in the field of physics. This book has several lab activities devoted to sound and vibrations that touch on the basic ideas. Instructions and explanations are abbreviated, compared with other books. Good general resource.

4. *Science Projects About Sound. Written by Robert Gardner. ISBN 1-7660-1166-6. Published by Enslow. 112 pages.*

Thirty-nine labs in 6 chapters is a bit deceiving because each lab has several extensions and additional ideas for you to try. The book is written for older kids who have a good grasp of their math skills. Mr. Gardner introduces simple formulas to calculate speed of sound. He presents some concepts about wave and wave properties. Great book for more advanced students, junior high or high school.

5. *Bangs and Twangs. Science Fun with Sound. Written by Vicki Cobb. Illustrated by Steve Haefele. ISBN 0-7613-1571-3. Published by The Millbrook Press, Inc. 48 pages.*

A very colorful book, full of fun ideas for kids and written in a format where the author narrates the text to the kid reading with the help of a mischievous alien by the name of Igor. Together, they walk the kids through seven lab activities and then extend them to the real world, tying it all together.

6. *Science For Fun: Hearing Sounds. Written by Gary Gibson. ISBN 1-56294-614-5. Published by Copper Beech Books. 32 pages.*

Twelve very fun activities written in a very busy, colorful manner produces lots of eye candy for young readers. As you work through each of the activities that is presented, the kids will get a good fundamental overview of sound and how sound is produced. They will make several great noise makers along the way. Great book for younger kids who are interested in science but love the rewards of making something that produces a funny and entertaining sound.

Develop an Original Idea

Step Two • Do the Lab

Choose a lab activity that looks interesting and try the experiment. Some kids make the mistake of thinking that all you have to do is find a lab in a book, repeat the lab, and you are on the gravy train with biscuit wheels. Your goal is to ask an ORIGINAL question, not repeat an experiment that has been done a bazillion times before.

As you do the lab, be thinking not only about the data you are collecting, but of ways you could adapt or change the experiment to find out new information. The point of the science fair project is to have you become an actual scientist and contribute a little bit of new knowledge to the world.

You know that they don't pay all of those engineers good money to sit around and repeat other people's lab work. The company wants new ideas, so if you are able to generate and explore new ideas, you become very valuable, not only to that company but to society. It is the question-askers that find cures for diseases, create new materials, figure out ways to make existing machines energy-efficient, and change the way that we live. For the purpose of illustration, we are going to take a lab titled, "Prisms, Water Prisms" from another book, *Photon U*, and run it through the rest of the process. The lab uses a tub of water, an ordinary mirror, and light to create a prism that splits the light into the spectrum of a rainbow. Cool. Easy to do. Not expensive and open to all kinds of adaptations, including the four that we discuss on the next page.

Step Three • *Bend, Fold, Spindle, & Mutilate Your Lab*

Once you have picked out an experiment, ask if it is possible to do any of the following things to modify it into an original experiment. You want to try and change the experiment to make it more interesting and find out one new, small piece of information.

Heat it	Freeze it	Reverse it	Double it
Bend it	Invert it	Poison it	Dehydrate it
Drown it	Stretch it	Fold it	Ignite it
Split it	Irradiate it	Oxidize it	Reduce it
Chill it	Speed it up	Color it	Grease it
Expand it	Substitute it	Remove it	Slow it down

If you take a look at our examples, that's exactly what we did to the main idea. We took the list of 24 different things that you could do to an experiment—not nearly all of them by the way—and tried a couple of them out on the prism setup.

Double it: Get a second prism and see if you can continue to separate the colors farther by lining up a second prism in the rainbow of the first.

Reduce it: Figure out a way to gather up the colors that have been produced and mix them back together to produce white light again.

Reverse it: Experiment with moving the flashlight and paper closer to the mirror and farther away. Draw a picture and be able to predict what happens to the size and clarity of the rainbow image.

Substitute it: You can also create a rainbow on a sunny day, using a garden hose with a fine-spray nozzle attached. Set the nozzle adjustment so that a fine mist is produced and move the mist around in the sunshine until you see the rainbow. This works better if the sun is lower in the sky; late afternoon is best.

Hypothesis Worksheet

Step Three (Expanded) • *Bend, Fold, Spindle Worksheet*
This worksheet will give you an opportunity to work through the process of creating an original idea.

A. Write down the lab idea that you want to mangle.

_____

_____

_____

_____

B. List the possible variables you could change in the lab.

i. _____

ii. _____

iii. _____

iv. _____

v. _____

C. Take one variable listed in section B and apply one of the 24 changes listed below to it. Write that change down and state your new lab idea in the space below. Do that with three more changes.

Heat it	Freeze it	Reverse it	Double it
Bend it	Invert it	Poison it	Dehydrate it
Drown it	Stretch it	Fold it	Ignite it
Split it	Irradiate it	Oxidize it	Reduce it
Chill it	Speed it up	Color it	Grease it
Expand it	Substitute it	Remove it	Slow it down

i. _____

_____

_____

_____

ii. _____

_____

_____

_____

iii. _____

_____

_____

_____

iv. _____

_____ STRETCHING! _____

_____

_____

Step Four • Create an Original Idea—Your Hypothesis
    Your hypothesis should be stated as an opinion. You've done
the basic experiment, you've made observations, you're not stupid.
Put two and two together and make a PREDICTION. Be sure that you
are experimenting with just a single variable.

    A. State your hypothesis in the space below. List the variable.
    i. _____

_____

_____

_____

    ii. Variable tested: _____

Sample Hypothesis Worksheet

On the previous two pages is a worksheet that will help you develop your thoughts and a hypothesis. Here is sample of the finished product to help you understand how to use it.

A. Write down the lab idea that you want to mutilate.
A mirror is placed in a tub of water. A beam of light is focused through the water onto the mirror, producing a rainbow on the wall.

B. List the possible variables you could change in the lab.
    i. **Source of light**
    ii. **The liquid in the tub**
    iii. **The distance from flashlight to mirror**

C. Take one variable listed in section B and apply one of the 24 changes to it. Write that change down and state your new lab idea in the space below.

The shape of the beam of light can be controlled by making and placing cardboard filters over the end of the flashlight. Various shapes such as circles, squares, and slits will produce different quality rainbows.

D. State your hypothesis in the space below. List the variable. Be sure that when you write the hypothesis you are stating an idea and <u>not asking a question.</u>

Hypothesis: The narrower the beam of light the tighter, brighter, and more focused the reflected rainbow will appear.

Variable tested: **The opening on the filter**

Scientific Method
• Step 2 •
Gather Information

Gather Information

Read about your topic and find out what we already know. Check books, videos, the Internet, and movies, talk with experts in the field, and molest an encyclopedia or two. Gather as much information as you can before you begin planning your experiment.

In particular, there are several things that you will want to pay special attention to and that should accompany any good science fair project.

A. Major Scientific Concepts

Be sure that you research and explain the main idea(s) that is/re driving your experiment. It may be a law of physics or chemical rule or an explanation of an aspect of plant physiology.

B. Scientific Words

As you use scientific terms in your paper, you should also define them in the margins of the paper or in a glossary at the end of the report. You cannot assume that everyone knows about geothermal energy transmutation in sulfur-loving bacteria. Be prepared to define some new terms for them... and scrub your hands really well when you are done if that is your project.

C. Historical Perspective

When did we first learn about this idea, and who is responsible for getting us this far? You need to give a historical perspective with names, dates, countries, awards, and other recognition.

Building a Research Foundation

1. This sheet is designed to help you organize your thoughts and give you some ideas on where to look for information on your topic. When you prepare your lab report, you will want to include the background information outlined below.

A. *Major Scientific Concepts (Two is plenty.)*

    i. _____

_____

_____

_____

    ii. _____

_____

_____

_____

B. *Scientific Words (No more than 10)*

    i. _____

    ii. _____

    iii. _____

    iv. _____

    v. _____

    vi. _____

    vii. _____

    viii. _____

    ix. _____

    x. _____

C. *Historical Perspective*
    Add this as you find it.

2. There are several sources of information that are available to help you fill in the details from the previous page.

A. *Contemporary Print Resources*
   (Magazines, Newspapers, Journals)

   i. _____

   ii. _____

   iii. _____

   iv. _____

   v. _____

   vi. _____

B. *Other Print Resources*
   (Books, Encyclopedias, Dictionaries, Textbooks)

   i. _____

   ii. _____

   iii. _____

   iv. _____

   v. _____

   vi. _____

C. *Celluloid Resources*
   (Films, Filmstrips, Videos)

   i. _____

   ii. _____

   iii. _____

   iv. _____

   v. _____

   vi. _____

D. Electronic Resources:
  (Internet Website Addresses, DVDs, MP3s)
    i. _____
    ii. _____
    iii. _____
    iv. _____
    v. _____
    vi. _____
    vii. _____
    viii. _____
    ix. _____
    x. _____

E. Human Resources
  (Scientists, Engineers, Professionals, Professors, Teachers)
    i. _____
    ii. _____
    iii. _____
    iv. _____
    v. _____
    vi. _____

You may want to keep a record of all of your research and add it to the back of the report as an Appendix. Some teachers who are into volume think this is really cool. Others, like myself, find it a pain in the tuchus. No matter what you do, be sure to keep an accurate record of where you find data. If you quote from a report word-for-word, be sure to give proper credit with either a footnote or parenthetical reference. This is very important for credibility and accuracy, and it will keep you out of trouble with plagiarism (copying without giving credit).

Scientific Method
• Step 3 •
Design Your Experiment

Acquire Your Lab Materials

The purpose of this section is to help you plan your experiment. You'll make a map of where you are going, how you want to get there, and what you will take along.

List the materials you will need to complete your experiment in the table below. Be sure to list multiples if you will need more than one item. Many science materials double as household items in their spare time. Check around the house before you buy anything from a science supply company or hardware store. For your convenience, we have listed some suppliers on page 19 of this book.

Material	Qty.	Source	$
1.			
2.			
3.			
4.			
5.			
6.			
7.			
8.			
9.			
10.			
11.			
12.			

Total $_____

Outline Your Experiment

This sheet is designed to help you outline your experiment. If you need more space, make a copy of this page to finish your outline. When you are done with this sheet, review it with an adult, make any necessary changes, review safety concerns on the next page, prepare your data tables, gather your equipment, and start to experiment.

In the space below, list what you are going to do in the order you are going to do it.

i. _____

_____

_____

_____

ii. _____

_____

_____

_____

iii. _____

_____

_____

_____

iv. _____

_____

_____

_____

v. _____

_____

_____

_____

Evaluate Safety Concerns

We have included an overall safety section in the front of this book on pages 16–18, but there are some very specific questions you need to ask, and prepare for, depending on the needs of your experiment. If you find that you need to prepare for any of these safety concerns, place a check mark next to the letter.

_____ *A. Goggles & Eyewash Station*
If you are mixing chemicals or working with materials that might splinter or produce flying objects, goggles and an eyewash station or sink with running water should be available.

_____ *B. Ventilation*
If you are mixing chemicals that could produce fire, smoke, fumes, or obnoxious odors, you will need to use a vented hood or go outside and perform the experiment in the fresh air.

_____ *C. Fire Blanket or Fire Extinguisher*
If you are working with potentially combustible chemicals or electricity, a fire blanket and extinguisher nearby are a must.

_____ *D. Chemical Disposal*
If your experiment produces a poisonous chemical or there are chemical-filled tissues (as in dissected animals), you may need to make arrangements to dispose of the by-products from your lab.

_____ *E. Electricity*
If you are working with materials and developing an idea that uses electricity, make sure that the wires are in good repair, that the electrical demand does not exceed the capacity of the supply, and that your work area is grounded.

_____ *F. Emergency Phone Numbers*
Look up and record the following phone numbers for the Fire Department: _____ , Poison Control: _____ , and Hospital: _____. Post them in an easy-to-find location.

Prepare Data Tables

Finally, you will want to prepare your data tables and have them ready to go before you start your experiment. Each data table should be easy to understand and easy for you to use.

A good data table has a **title** that describes the information being collected, and it identifies the **variable** and the **unit** being collected on each data line. The variable is *what* you are measuring and the unit is *how* you are measuring it. They are usually written like this:

Variable (unit), or to give you some examples:

Time (seconds)
Distance (meters)
Electricity (volts)

An example of a well-prepared data table looks like the sample below. We've cut the data table into thirds because the book is too small to display the whole line.

Determining the Boiling Point of Compound X_1

Time (min.)	0	1	2	3	4	5	6
Temp. (°C)							

Time (min.)	7	8	9	10	11	12	13
Temp. (°C)							

Time (min.)	14	15	16	17	18	19	20
Temp. (°C)							

Scientific Method
• Step 4 •
Conduct the Experiment

Lab Time

It's time to get going. You've generated a hypothesis, collected the materials, written out the procedure, checked the safety issues, and prepared your data tables. Fire it up. Here's the short list of things to remember as you experiment.

_____ *A. Follow the Procedure, Record Any Changes*
Follow your own directions specifically as you wrote them. If you find the need to change the procedure once you are into the experiment, that's fine; it's part of the process. Make sure to keep detailed records of the changes. When you repeat the experiment a second or third time, follow the new directions exactly.

_____ *B. Observe Safety Rules*
It's easier to complete the lab activity if you are in the lab rather than the emergency room.

_____ *C. Record Data Immediately*
Collect temperatures, distances, voltages, revolutions, and any other variables and immediately record them into your data table. Do not think you will be able to remember them and fill everything in after the lab is completed.

_____ *D. Repeat the Experiment Several Times*
The more data that you collect, the better. It will give you a larger data base and your averages will be more meaningful. As you do multiple experiments, be sure to identify each data set by date and time so you can separate them out.

_____ *E. Prepare for Extended Experiments*
Some experiments require days or weeks to complete, particularly those with plants and animals or the growing of crystals. Prepare a safe place for your materials so your experiment can continue undisturbed while you collect the data. Be sure you've allowed enough time for your due date.

Scientific Method
• Step 5 •
Collect and Display Data

Types of Graphs

This section will give you some ideas on how you can display the information you are going to collect as a graph. A graph is simply a picture of the data that you gathered portrayed in a manner that is quick and easy to reference. There are four kinds of graphs described on the next two pages. If you find you need a leg up in the graphing department, we have a book in the series called *Data Tables & Graphing*. It will guide you through the process.

Line and Bar Graphs

These are the most common kinds of graphs. The most consistent variable is plotted on the "x", or horizontal, axis and the more temperamental variable is plotted along the "y", or vertical, axis. Each data point on a line graph is recorded as a dot on the graph and then all of the dots are connected to form a picture of the data. A bar graph starts on the horizontal axis and moves up to the data line.

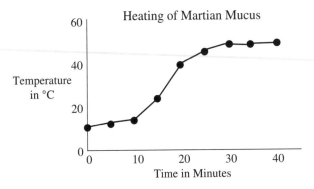

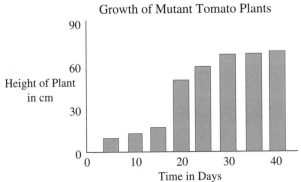

Catch a Wave • Winholtz, Cramer, Twyman, & Hixson

Best Fit Graphs

A best fit graph was created to show averages or trends rather than specific data points. The data that has been collected is plotted on a graph just as on a line graph, but instead of drawing a line from point to point to point, which sometimes is impossible anyway, you just free hand a line that hits "most of the data."

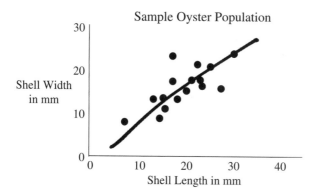

Pie Graphs

Pie graphs are used to show relationships between different groups. All of the data is totaled up and a percentage is determined for each group. The pie is then divided to show the relationship of one group to another.

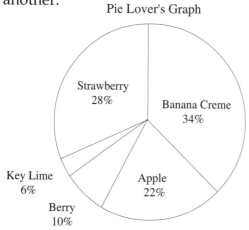

Other Kinds of Data

1. Written Notes & Observations

This is the age-old technique used by all scientists. Record your observations in a lab book. Written notes can be made quickly as the experiment is proceeding, and they can then be expounded upon later. Quite often notes made in the heat of an experiment are revisited during the evaluation portion of the process, and they can shed valuable light on how or why the experiment went the way it did.

2. Drawings

Quick sketches as well as fully developed drawings can be used as a way to report data for a science experiment. Be sure to title each drawing and, if possible, label what it is that you are looking at. Drawings that are actual size are best.

3. Photographs, Videotapes, and Audiotapes

Usually better than drawings, quicker, and more accurate, but you do have the added expense and time of developing the film. However, they can often capture images and details that are not usually seen by the naked eye.

4. The Experiment Itself

Some of the best data you can collect and present is the actual experiment itself. Nothing will speak more effectively for you than the plants you grew, the specimens you collected, or that big pile of tissue that was an armadillo you peeled from the tread of an 18-wheeler.

Scientific Method
· Step 6 ·
Present Your Ideas

Oral Report Checklist

It is entirely possible that you will be asked to make an oral presentation to your classmates. This will give you an opportunity to explain what you did and how you did it. Quite often this presentation is part of your overall score, so if you do well, it will enhance your chances for one of the bigger awards.

To prepare for your oral report, your science fair presentation should include the following components:

Physical Display

_____a.   freestanding display board
                 hypothesis
                 data tables, graphs, photos, etc.
                 abstract (short summary)
_____b.   actual lab setup (equipment)

Oral Report

_____a.   hypothesis or question
_____b.   background information
                 concepts
                 word definitions
                 history or scientists
_____c.   experimental procedure
_____d.   data collected
                 data tables
                 graphs
                 photos or drawings
_____e.   conclusions and findings
_____f.   ask for questions

Set the display board up next to you on the table. Transfer the essential information to index cards. Use the index cards for reference, but do not read from them. Speak in a clear voice, hold your head up, and make eye contact with your peers. Ask if there are any questions before you finish and sit down.

Written Report Checklist

Next up is the written report, also called your lab write-up. After you compile or sort the data you have collected during the experiment and evaluate the results, you will be able to come to a conclusion about your hypothesis. Remember, disproving an idea is as valuable as proving it.

This sheet is designed to help you write up your science fair project and present your data in an organized manner. This is a final checklist for you.

To prepare your write-up, your science fair report should include the following components:

_____ a.   binder
_____ b.   cover page, title, & your name
_____ c.   abstract (one paragraph summary)
_____ d.   table of contents with page numbers
_____ e.   hypothesis or question
_____ f.   background information
        concepts
        word definitions
        history or scientists
_____ g.   list of materials used
_____ h.   experimental procedure
        written description
        photo or drawing of setup
_____ i.   data collected
        data tables
        graphs
        photos or drawings
_____ j.   conclusions and findings
_____ k.   glossary of terms
_____ l.   references

Display Checklist

2. Prepare your display to accompany the report. A good display should include the following:

Freestanding Display

_____	a.	freestanding cardboard back
_____	b.	title of experiment
_____	c.	your name
_____	d.	hypothesis
_____	e.	findings of the experiment
_____	f.	photo or illustrations of equipment
_____	g.	data tables or graphs

Additional Display Items

_____	h.	a copy of the write-up
_____	i.	actual lab equipment setup

Glossary,
Index,
and
More Ideas

Glossary

Air Burst Rockets

A cool new rocket that is launched using air and water. A combination of membranes and pressure allow you shoot the rocket over a thousand feet in the air. So why is it in a book on sound? The water leaves the rocket in excess of the speed of sound and produces a mini sonic boom.

Amplification

Increasing the loudness of the sound produced or received. In the case of producing sound, the waves can be focused by a megaphone or other device. In the case of receiving, talk with an elephant.

Buzzers

Annoying electrical devices that use electricity to vibrate thin pieces of plastic. Vibrations produce sounds, but no one said that it would be fun to listen to those sounds for any length of time.

Chicken in a Cup

Don't call the PETA folks. This is a string attached to a wax cup. When the string is pulled while it is wet, it produces a squawk that is remarkably similar to a chicken clucking. No real live chickens are harmed or even used for this lab activity.

Convection Carafe

A large, metal tube with a piece of metal screen stuffed in one end is heated with a propane torch. The screen gets red hot, the tube is removed from the flame, and the tube begins to hum. Grateful that it is no longer being heated? No, a standing wave is set up by the convective air moving through the tube.

Doppler Effect

Sound waves produced by a moving object. The faster the object moves toward you, the closer the sound waves are that are produced, giving the illusion of a high-pitched sound. As the object passes, the distance between the waves lengthens, and the sound appears to get lower in pitch.

Explosions

Any time air is rapidly heated or compressed, it sends a shock wave out that is interpreted by our ears as an explosion.

Frequency

A sound wave is measured by the number or beats or pulses it produces per second. The more pulses, the higher the frequency and the higher the pitch of the sound that is produced. By the same contrast, the slower the frequency of the sound wave, the lower the pitch is that is produced.

Gramophone

What you use to call your granny ... sorry, couldn't resist. An old-fashioned record player. RCA corporation uses it in its logo (the dog sitting with one ear cocked into the cone). It was the great granddaddy to the modern day phonograph.

Guitar

A box with strings. The strings vibrate when struck, strummed, or plucked, and the box amplifies the sound produced. Not very romantic, but this is science.

Kazoo

The noise some people make when they sneeze. Nope, just checking to see if you were paying attention. A tube with a hole cut into the top-center section. The hole is covered with plastic. When you hum into the tube, the hum is amplified by the plastic coating. Considered possible source of migraine headaches for elementary music teachers.

Matter

All material known to man is lumped in one big category called matter. It is generally found to exist in three different states, solid, liquid, and gas. Sound, the topic we are currently studying, has the ability to pass through all three states of matter.

Glossary

Megaphone
A large cone that you hold to your mouth if you wish to express yourself to a large group of people, or a cone that you hold to your ear if your tympanic membrane is as taut as a bowl of Jello.

Morse Code
A simple code developed by Samuel Morse to be used over the telegraph. It consists of a series of dots and/or dashes that represent letters of the alphabet or numbers.

Oscilloscope
A scientific instrument that collects sound wave information and portrays it as a graph or picture that can be easily interpreted by human eyes.

PVC Orchestra
Not a real orchestra, but you probably guessed that by now. PVC stands for polyvinyl chloride. It is a hard plastic material that is used to make, among other things, sprinkler pipe. If the pipe is cut to specified lengths and whapped on the palm of the hand, it produces a variety of sounds. It is possible that actual tunes could be recognized.

Pitch
The word that describes how high or how low the sound made by a particular instrument will sound to the ears. If the instrument is short, it produces a high frequency and the pitch will also be high. If the instrument is long, the pitch will be low.

Poppers
Paper that has been folded into a flexible triangle shape. When the instrument is given a quick, downward flick, the paper unfolds and snaps. This produces a "pop."

Rain Stick

A hollow stick or tube that has had numerous nails driven through the center. The tube is filled with popcorn kernels or pebbles and both ends are capped. When the tube is held vertically, the pebbles fall from one end of the tube to the other, bouncing off the nails. This creates the illusion of the sound of rain falling from the sky.

Resonance

Every wave has a particular length. When a container matches the length of the wave, the wave is amplified and sounds much louder than it would in other sized instruments. When this happens, scientists call it finding the resonant length. If a container matches the sound wave produced in a room, it will also resonate.

Singing Rods

Solid aluminum rods that are rubbed with rosin. When the rods are held at their nodal points, usually the middle or the one-quarter spot, and the rods are rubbed, they begin to vibrate. In fact, if you match the speed of the rubbing with the frequency of the wave, you can set up a resonant, standing wave, which is very loud and obnoxious.

Soda Cannon

If baking soda is mixed with vinegar in a stoppered tube, the combination is usually sufficient to cause an explosion. The explosion is produced when the chemicals react to make carbon dioxide. The gas builds up inside the tube and when the stopper is eventually shoved out of the tube, the rapidly expanding gas creates shock waves.

Sonic Boom

Sound waves travel through air at about 620 miles per hour. If an object moves faster than that the sound waves pile up on one another and a sonic boom is produced. It sounds like a loud explosion similar to the kind of compression that is caused by a chemical explosion (dynamite or some other kind of explosive).

Glossary

Sound Production
Sound can be converted from many other sources of energy including electricity, motion, heat, lights, and chemical reactions.

Sound Proofing
Coating or covering a material so that it absorbs, rather than reflects the sound waves that strike its surface.

Soup Can Telephone
Connect a string between two empty, clean soup can and you can talk to someone across the room and have them understand you. Your vocal chords produce sound waves which vibrate the metal in the can. The metal in the can vibrates a string which is passed to the other can and voila, your in the phone business.

Stethoscope
An instrument that is used to collect sound vibrations from the human body. Most notably the heart but also the lungs.

s' Trombones
Our silly name for an instrument made out of two straws. A thin straw is placed inside a fatter straw. As you blow on the thin straw, which has been modified, it vibrates producing sound. The second straw allows you to manipulate the length and therefore the pitch of the instrument.

Thunder Drums
A large cone with a thin spring attached to the bottom. When it is shaken it sounds like distant thunder rolling over the countryside.

Tuning Fork
A piece of metal that looks like a tall skinny "U" attached to a handle. When the "U" is tapped, it vibrates at a specified frequency. Used in lots of experiments, this provides an excellent way to demonstrate that sound is produced by vibrations.

Vacuum

Nothing. No matter whatsoever. Space is a vacuum, and because sound needs something to bump into to travel from place to place, it cannot travel through space. Kind of messes with all those cool space movies, doesn't it?

Vibration

The repetitive movement of an object, back and forth, up and down, in a circular motion. When an object vibrates, it can produce a sound frequency that we may be able to hear. The larger the vibrations, the louder the sound; the faster the vibrations, the higher the pitch of the sound. This is really at the heart of what sound is.

Water Whistle

Fill a straw full of water. Blow across the top of the straw and produce a whistling sound. Let the water fall out of the straw while you are whistling, and the pitch drops. Water whistle, take a bow.

Waves, Compression

Waves that travel in horizontal herds. If you squish a Slinky spring together and let it go, the wave travels down the spring as a moving clump of coils. That is a wave composed of compressed coils. Air does the same thing, as do vibrations in other kinds of metal.

Waves, Transverse

This is the traditional wave-model wave. It looks like a wave on the water. It goes up and then down and then up again. It consists of nodes, antinodes, troughs, and frequencies.

Index

Index

Notes

Notes

More Science Books

Gravity Works
50 hands-on lab activities from the world of things that fly. Air, air pressure, Bernoulli's law, and all things that fly, float, or glide.

Thermodynamic Thrills
50 hands-on lab activities that investigate heat via conduction, convection, radiation, specific heat, and temperature.

Newton Take 3
50 hands-on lab activities that explore the world of mechanics, forces, gravity, and Newton's three laws of motion.

n U
activities
of light.
ic col-
and
o-
V

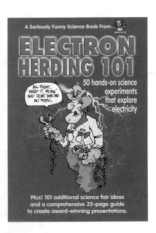

Electron Herding 101
50 hands-on lab activities that introduce static electricity, circuit electricity, and include a number of fun, and very easy-to-build projects.

Opposites Attract
50 hands-on lab activities that delve into the world of natural and man-made magnets as well as the characteristics of magnetic attraction.